W9-CIR-116

Guide For Translators

by Morry Sofer

Schreiber Publishing, Rockville, Maryland
A Division of Schreiber Translations, Inc.

Guide for Translators
by Morry Sofer
Published by:

S T I   **Schreiber Publishing**
Post Office Box 2142
Rockville, MD 20847 U.S.A.

Copyright © 1995 by Schreiber Translations, Inc.

First Printing 1995

Publisher's Cataloging in Publication

Sofer, Morry.
    Guide for Translators / by Morry Sofer.
    p. cm.
    Includes index.
    Preassigned LCCN: 95-69772.
    ISBN 1-887563-02-4
    1. Translating and interpreting--Handbooks, manuals etc. I. Title.
    P306.S64 1995   418'.02
                     QBI95-20273

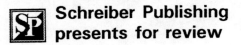 **Schreiber Publishing presents for review**

Title: **Guide for Translators**
Author: Morry Sofer
Edition: First
LCCN: 95-69772
ISBN: 1-887563-02-4
Pages: 128, 5.5 x 8.5
Price: $19.95
Season: Fall
Publication date: September 1995

The book will be featured at the annual conference of the American Translators Association in Nashville, Tennessee, in November 1995. An experimental version of the book has been used successfully for training translators since 1993.

A copy of your review to the address below would be appreciated.

Schreiber Publishing
P.O. Box 2142
Rockville, MD 20847
Tel. 301/816-0557
Fax: 301/816-2398

GUIDE FOR TRANSLATORS

Table of Contents

1.	The Purpose of This Guide	1
2.	A Brief History of Translation	4
3.	Basic Requisites for Becoming a Professional Translator	9
4.	The Well-Rounded Translator	14
5.	Good and Bad Translation Habits	16
6.	Translation Techniques	19
7.	Translation Equipment	24
8.	Dictionaries and Reference Literature	27
9.	How to Operate Successfully As a Freelance Translator	30
10.	Where to Find Work	34
11.	Seeking a Translation Career	40
12.	Training Programs	43
13.	Oral Interpretation	45
14.	Machine Translation	47
15.	Translation: A Life-Long Career	49

Appendix 1: Dictionaries — 51
Arabic — 56
Chinese — 58
French — 62
German — 65
Hebrew — 69
Italian — 71
Japanese — 73
Portuguese — 75
Russian — 77
Spanish — 81
Appendix 2: Dictionary Sources — 85
Appendix 3: Sources of Translation Work — 88
Appendix 4: Translation Courses and Programs — 110
Appendix 5: Translator Accreditation — 117
Translation Glossary — 118
Index — 121

ACKNOWLEDGEMENT

Jorge Perez, former Deputy Chief, Language Services, U.S. Department of State, gave me my first break in this business. Sixteen years later, he helped me with the Spanish version of the self-training program attached to this guide. Profound thanks!

Marla Schulman encouraged me to pursue this project, and relieved me of several duties so that I could bring it to fruition. Irina Knizhnik provided invaluable help with the assessment of the Russian, Chinese and Japanese dictionaries.
Kathy Biancaniello helped with the format and the technical consulting on electronic media.
Rachel Schreiber designed the cover.

Finally, a word of thanks to the hundreds of colleagues, past and present, from whom I learned everything I know about translation, one of the most exciting vocations I have ever had the privilege to pursue.

M.S.

1. THE PURPOSE OF THIS GUIDE

Many people assume that any literate person who knows more than one language can translate. Nothing is farther from the truth. Translation is a talent few people possess, although many think they do. Without an innate aptitude for translation, one can go through the motions of replacing words with their equivalents in another language, but the results are likely to fall short of the intent and flavor of the original. Let me be quick to add that even the best translation is never a full and true reflection of its source, simply because no two languages in the world, not even the most closely related, are identical in their way of using words and nuances. The best one can hope for is a rendition close enough to the original not to alter any of its meaning, full enough not to omit any detail, no matter how seemingly insignificant, and elegant enough to at least provide some of the stylistic character of the original text.

Precisely because there is no such thing as a perfect translation of an original source, translation is always a challenge which requires skill, training and experience. The purpose of this guide is to help those who know at least two languages and have an aptitude for translating take the necessary steps to sharpen their skills through training and practice, and hopefully go on to start acquiring the experience necessary to become a truly productive and effective translator.

This guide is the result of my 30 years of translation experience, including literary translation with several book translations to my credit, later on as a technical translator for U.S. Government agencies, and, since 1983, as the founder and president of a translation service which engages hundreds of translators in over 50 different languages throughout the United States and abroad.

During the last ten years I have witnessed a dramatic change in the role of translators in this country and around the world. The opportunities for translators are growing like never before.

This is due to the fact that the "global village" idea is becoming a fact of life with every passing day, thanks to the disappearance of the Iron Curtain, multinational alliances like the European Community, the growing global role of the United Nations, the globalization of business, and the miracle of communications. Such tools as the fax and the modem enable translators to receive text which was sent, say, from Washington to Athens by fax, translate it, and send it back to Washington over the modem, all at an affordable cost and without wasting any valuable time in transit.

Last but not least, the constant improvements in the computer field have tripled and quadrupled the output of the professional translator, and have made the task of translating much easier. It is quite clear that computers will play an even greater role in the translation field in years to come, making translation more affordable and widely used. (A word of caution: those who maintain that computers will soon replace human translators altogether are not familiar with all the facts. The general consensus among the experts today is that computer technology will continue to enhance translation, but only as an aid rather than a replacement of human translation).

Thousands of students in American colleges and universities major in foreign languages. Many of them wonder what to do with their degree once they graduate. Many consider the possibilities of translation, only to find out there is little opportunity to break into this field, since there seems to be a gap between the formal education stage and the professional stage of working as a trained or accredited translator.

The purpose of this guide is to bridge this gap by providing information which, combined with a training program designed to help improve the aspiring translator's skills, will provide the necessary preparation for a professional translation career. The guide is designed to point you in the right direction. The rest is up to you. Once you begin to pursue your own translation career, you will start formulating your own guidelines, develop your own techniques, and be ever on the lookout for new words, new knowledge, new linguistic sources, and a better understanding of how to communicate words and ideas, which, after all, is what translation is all about.

2. A BRIEF HISTORY OF TRANSLATION

Translation is one of the oldest occupations in the world. One of the earliest dictionaries known to us was discovered a few years ago by Italian archeologists in the ancient town of Ebla, in the Middle East. It dates back anywhere between 6,000 and 10,000 years, to the dawn of civilization. It is chiseled in clay tablets, in a writing (actually chiseling) method known as cuneiform. There, on the face of the tablet, are two parallel columns of words, in two different ancient tongues, related to taxation (yes, tax-collecting is also one of the oldest occupations).

Before there was writing there was speaking. Neighboring tribes and nations have always spoken different dialects and even totally different languages. And yet they had to talk to each other in order to engage in trade, to threaten each other, and, after the folly of fighting was over, to talk peace. And so they needed oral interpreters, those linguistically gifted individuals who managed to master one or more tongues other than their own. From the beginning of time, those interpreters were considered an important asset for the community, or for the leader of the tribe or nation. They played a vital role in both trade and in the affairs of state. Quite often, they became confidants of the ruler, and enjoyed special privileges.

There was, however, a downside to the life of the interpreter. Since the interpreter was often at the center of important events, taking part in crucial negotiations and decisions, if things went wrong, if a deal failed, or, worse yet, a battle lost, the interpreter was often used as a scapegoat. Examples of this unfortunate turn of events abound throughout the history of interpretation as well as translation.

Writing, as was mentioned before, has been around for at least 10,000 years, probably longer. In ancient Egypt, the court scribe was one of the most important officers of the Pharaoh's court. He was a highly cultivated person, and most likely knew more than one language. In the Old Testament there is no clear distinction between the scribe and the interpreter or translator. When the Assyrians lay siege to Jerusalem, a Hebrew scribe serves as an interpreter between the Hebrew-speaking Judeans and their Aramean-speaking enemies.

Civilization as we know it today would have never evolved without translators. At every critical juncture in history, when one civilization went into decline and another one emerged, the role of the translator became critical, enabling the new emerging civilization to benefit from the cultural gains of the older one, and incorporate them into the fabric of the new culture. Thus, when Rome became the dominant culture of the ancient world, it translated the work of the Greek philosophers, poets and scientists into Latin, and built its entire culture on their teachings. When Christianity began to evolve during the decline of the Roman Empire, its scholars translated the Old Testament into Latin (the Vulgate). These translations became the cornerstone of Christendom, along with the teachings of ancient Greece and Rome.

During the Middle Ages much of the teaching of the ancients was suppressed by the Church, and translation became a highly restricted function. Meanwhile, Islam emerged as a new vigorous cultural force, creating new philosophy, science and literature. While Christian Europe sank into backwardness, Islam, in both the Middle East and in Spain, encouraged translation as part of the intercultural process that helps civilizations grow and prosper. It was precisely in Islamic Spain that translation experienced a Golden Age unlike anything before or after in recorded history. In the city of Toledo, in the heart of the Iberian Peninsula, Arabic, Jewish, and later Christian translators labored for years, translating many Greek, Roman, Arabic, Hebrew and other classics into the new languages of Europe -- Spanish, French, German, Italian, English and so on. These translations opened the doors of civilization to a new age known as the Renaissance, which would usher in the modern

5

world as we know it today.

For the English-speaking world, perhaps the most crucial cultural event ever was the translation of the Bible into English, popularly known as the King James version. Equally critical for German culture was the translation of the Bible into German by Martin Luther. The King James version was a religious as well as a cultural turning point in the history of English civilization. Indeed, for the Church, for the modern state, and for all of culture and science, translation became since the Renaissance and down to our own time a most critical function of promoting, disseminating and sharing ideas, beliefs, great drama, poetry and prose, and the new advances of science, across linguistic barriers.

During the age of the Great Discoveries, great explorers such as Columbus, Pizarro, Cortés and others came in contact with new, hitherto unknown cultures and languages, those of the natives of the New World and other parts of the globe. Here again interpreters became the bridge between the White man and the other races. Cortés, the conqueror of Mexico, might have failed in his ruthless mission had it not been for a local native woman who served as his interpreter. The same was true of many other conquerors and discoverers. The great civilization of the ancient Maya of Central America was made known to us through the translation into Spanish of such Mayan classics as the *Popol Vu*.

The conquest of new worlds by the nations of Europe did not, however, result in an attitude of respect on the part of the conquerors towards the conquered, whereby the languages of the latter might have been studied by the former, and their oral or written traditions translated into such languages as Spanish, English, French and so on. Instead, the colonizers looked upon their new subjects as heathens whose language and culture were worthless, and imposed their own language, culture and religion on those who survived the many massacres inflicted upon them by their enlightened conquerors. It won't be until many years later that valuable cultural assets, such as Indian dialects of North America, African languages, and many other oral and written traditions, will be treated with respect, studied, and translated, as is finally beginning to happen in our time, in some cases after the originators of those cultures have all but disappeared.

Thus, by the nineteenth century, Latin America became dominated by the Spanish language and culture, North America by English, with the exception of French in the province of Quebec, much of Africa by a variety of European tongues, and so on. Translation, up until World War II, became to a large extent the domain of the dominant European powers, promoting their various national interests.

All of this is finally beginning to change now, at the end of the twentieth century. We are finally standing on the threshold of a new golden age for translation, not unlike the one in Spain at the end of the Middle Ages. There is a new cultural openness in today's world, brought about by several factors, the most notable being the end of the Cold War between the West and the former Communist Bloc, the incredible progress in global communications, including such technologies as satellite communications, computers, modem, fax, e-mail and so on, and the fast-growing international trade throughout the entire world, as well as the new international awareness of many languages and cultures that for centuries were subjugated and suppressed. The world today, rather than being dominated by a few colonialist languages such as French, English or Spanish, is finally reaching a stage of linguistic and cultural - albeit not quite yet social and economic - equality, whereby literally hundreds of languages and dialects are beginning to play a part in the global tapestry of human interaction. As a result, hundreds of new dictionaries are being published all over the world, language courses are being offered everywhere in an unprecedented number of languages, and the demand for competent translators is growing at a steady rate.

In conclusion, as the twenty-first century is about to begin, the role of the translator will once again, as happened before during ancient and pre-modern history, become critical in shaping history and helping civilization make the transition into the next age.

Translators put a "spin" on history:

What was Adam and Eve's phone number?

Two-eight-(ate?)-one-apple

What did God tell Moses to take for his headache?

Two tablets.

Why did Columbus go to Cuba instead of India?

He figured it would be easier to go to a Spanish-speaking country.

---

3. BASIC REQUISITES FOR BECOMING A PROFESSIONAL TRANSLATOR

Any person who knows more than one language has the ability to explain a word or a sentence in what translators call "the source language" (the language you translate from) by using an equivalent word or sentence in what they call "the target language" (the language you translate into). This, in effect, is the beginning of translation. But it is only the beginning. It does not automatically turn a person into an accomplished translator. Along with the knowledge of the source and the target language, a translator must have an aptitude for translation. Years of experience have shown that some people are endowed with a talent for translation. It is not an acquired skill, like riding a bicycle. It is rather a talent, like playing the violin. Some people have it and some don't. It is not necessarily an indication of a lower or higher IQ. Nor is it an indication of how linguistically gifted one is. It is an inborn skill that enables a person to quickly and accurately change a text from one language into another, or, if you will, think in more than one language at the same time. If you possess this skill, then it behooves you to develop it and make use of it, because there is never an overabundance of good translators, and it is almost axiomatic that the good ones can always find either full-time or part-time work.

The **first** requisite for the working translator is a thorough knowledge of both the source and the target language. There is no point billing oneself as a translator if one is not fully familiar with both languages, or does not possess a vocabulary in both equal to that of a speaker of those languages who has a university education or its equivalent.

The **second** requisite is thorough "at-homeness" in both cultures. A language is a living phenomenon. It does not exist apart from the culture where it is spoken and written. It communicates not only the names of objects and different kinds of action, but also feelings, attitudes, beliefs, and so on. To be fully familiar with a language, one must also be familiar with the culture in which the language is used, indeed, with the people who use it, their ways, manners, beliefs and all that goes into making a culture.

Third, one must keep up with the growth and change of the language, and be up-to-date on all of its nuances and neologisms. Languages are in a constant state of flux, and words change meaning from year to year. A pejorative term can become laudatory, and a neutral term can become loaded with meaning. Thirty years ago the English word "gay" simply meant joyous. Now it is used to define an entire segment of society. We once spoke of the "almighty dollar." Now as we travel abroad we may find out the dollar is not necessarily everyone's preferred currency.

Fourth, a distinction must be made between the languages one translates from and into. Generally speaking, one translates from another language into one's own native language. This is because one is usually intimately familiar with one's own language, while even years of study and experience do not necessarily enable one to be completely at home with an acquired language. The exceptions to this rule are usually those people who have lived in more than one culture, and have spoken more than one language on a regular basis. Those may be able to translate in both directions. There are also rare gifted individuals who have mastered another language to such a degree that they can go both ways. They are indeed extremely rare. Given all of this, one should allow for the fact that while the ability of the accomplished translator to write and speak in the target language (i.e., one's native tongue) may be flawless, that person may not necessarily be able to write excellent prose or give great speeches in the source language (i.e., the language from which one translates). Then again, it is not necessary to be able to write and speak well in the language one translates from, while it is to be expected that a good translator is also a good writer and speaker in his or her native language.

Fifth, a professional translator has to be able to translate in more than one area of knowledge. Most professional translators are called upon to translate in a variety of fields. It is not uncommon for a translator to cover as many as twenty or thirty fields of knowledge in one year, including such areas as political subjects, economics, law, medicine, communications and so on. Obviously, it would be hard to find a translator who is an economist, a lawyer, a medical doctor, and an engineer all wrapped into one. In fact, such a person probably does not exist. One does not have to be a lawyer to translate legal documents. Many a professional translator has been able to gain enough knowledge and acquire a vocabulary in a variety of technical fields to be able to produce perfectly accurate and well written translations in those fields. This is not nearly as difficult as it may seem, since most technical fields utilize a well-defined number of terms which keep repeating themselves, and as one keeps translating the same subject, they become more and more familiar to the translator. One must, however, have a natural curiosity about many different areas of human knowledge and activity, and an interest in increasing one's vocabulary in a variety of related as well as unrelated fields.

Sixth, an effective translator must have a facility for writing or speaking (depending on whether the method used is writing, speaking, or dictation), and the ability to articulate quickly and accurately, either orally or in writing. Like a reporter, a translator must be able to transmit ideas in real time, and in good understandable language. Translation is a form of writing and speech-making, and a translator is, in a sense, a writer and an orator.

Seventh, a professional translator must develop a good speed of translation. There are two reasons for this: First, most clients wait until the last minute to assign a translation job. As a result, they turn to a translator or a translation service with what is perhaps the most typical question in this business: How soon can you have this job ready for me? The professional translator has to be prepared to accept that long job with the short turnaround time, or there will be no repeat business from that particular client or from most other clients, for that matter. Secondly, translation is generally paid by the word. The more words one can translate per hour, the more income one will generate. Translating 50 words per hour can land a translator in the poorhouse. Serious translation starts at 250 words per hour, and can reach as high as 1000 words per hour using word processing, and close to 3000 words per hour using dictation. High volume translators are the ones who will be the most successful.

Eighth, a translator must develop research skills, and be able to acquire reference sources which are essential for producing high quality translation. Without such sources even the best of translators cannot hope to be able to handle a large variety of subjects in many unrelated fields. Dedicated translators are the ones who are always on the lookout for new reference sources, and over time develop a data bank which can be used in their work.

Ninth, today's translator cannot be a stranger to hardware, software, fax, modem, and the latest developments in all those media. Translation has become completely dependent on electronic tools. Gone are the days of the typewriter, handwriting, and all the other "pre-historic" means of communication. The more one becomes involved in translation, the more one finds oneself caught up in the latest high-tech developments.

Tenth, a translator who wishes to be busy on a fairly regular basis doing translation work, must carefully consider the fact that certain languages are in high demand, say, in Washington or in Los Angeles, while others are not. Thus, for example, there is high demand for Japanese, German, Spanish, French, Chinese, Arabic, Russian and Italian in both Washington and

Some Common Misconceptions about Translation and Translators

1. Anyone with two years of high school language (or anyone who lived in another country for three years during early childhood) can translate.
2. There's no difference between translation, transcription, and transliteration.
3. A good translator doesn't need any reference literature.
4. Translators will soon be replaced by computers.
5. Translators don't need to know how to spell, since they can use the spell checker on their computer.
6. A good translator gets it right the first time, without any editing or proofreading.
7. Good translators are a dime a dozen.
8. If you can type in a foreign language then you are an accomplished translator.
9. Translators can translate both ways just as easily.
10. A 100-page technical manual that took four months and three persons to write, can be translated into another language by one translator in two days.

Los Angeles, but not nearly as much for Bulgarian, Farsi, Czech, or Afrikaans. If your language falls within the second group, it is extremely advisable to also have language expertise in one of the languages of the first group, or seriously consider whether your particular language has enough of a demand to warrant a major investment of time and effort on your part. One should always check and see what kind of a potential one's language specialty has in a given geographic area.

The above ten points are the essential criteria for developing a translation career. There are many other considerations, but none as important. If you feel that you can meet all of the above ten, then you should continue reading this guide and putting it to good use.

4. THE WELL-ROUNDED TRANSLATOR

The main division in the translation field is between literary and technical translation. Literary translation, which covers such areas as fiction, poetry, drama, and the humanities in general, is often done by writers of the same genre who actually author works of the same kind in the target language, or at least by translators with the required literary aptitude. For practical reasons, this guide will not cover literary translation, but instead will focus on the other major area of translation, namely, the technical. High quality literary translation has always been the domain of the few, and is hardly lucrative (don't even think of doing literary translation if your motive is money), while technical translation is done by a much greater number of practitioners, and is an ever-growing and expanding field with excellent earning opportunities. This chapter discusses the characteristics of the well-rounded technical translator.

The term "technical" is extremely broad. In the translation business it covers much more than technical subjects in the narrow sense of the word. In fact, there is an overlap between literary and technical translation, when it comes to such areas as social sciences, political subjects, and many other areas.

One way of defining technical translation is by asking the question, does the subject being translated require a specialized vocabulary, or is the language non-specialized? If the text being translated includes specialized terms in a given field, then the translation is technical.

The more areas (and languages) a translator can cover, the greater the opportunity for developing a successful translation career. Furthermore, as one becomes proficient in several areas, it becomes easier to add more. Besides, many technical areas are interrelated, and proficiency in one increases proficiency in another. In addition, every area breaks down into many sub-areas, each with its own vocabulary and its own linguistic idiosyncracies. Thus, for example, translating in Arabic does not make one an expert in all spoken Arabic dialects, yet a knowledge of several of those dialects is very beneficial for the professional Arabic translator.

How does one become a well-rounded translator? The answer can be summed up in one word - experience. One learns by doing, and the more one does the more well-rounded one becomes. The key to effective translation is practice. Since human knowledge grows day by day, and since language keeps growing and changing, the well-rounded translator must keep in touch with knowledge and language on a regular basis. The worst thing that can happen to a translator is to be out of touch with the source language for more than a couple of years. What the rusty translator may find out is that new words, new concepts and new ways of using those words and applying those concepts have come into being during that period of "hibernation," and one's old expertise is no longer reliable.

Translation, therefore, is a commitment one makes not for a limited period of time, but rather long-term. It is to be assumed that anyone who becomes a translator is the kind of person who loves words and loves the challenge of using words effectively and correctly. Such a person will not become an occasional translator, but will make translation a life-long practice.

5. GOOD AND BAD TRANSLATION HABITS

The accomplished translator can develop good as well as bad habits. Starting with the bad, we have already pointed out one - losing touch with the source language for long periods of time. Another bad habit is taking illegitimate shortcuts while translating. There are several types of such shortcuts. The most typical is failing to look up a word one is really not sure how to translate. Being ninety percent sure of a word's meaning is not good enough in professional translation. If one is not sure of a word's meaning, even after all available means have been exhausted, then one must put in a translator's note to that effect, or make it known in some other way that there is a problem with translating that particular word. Anything less will be deceptive.

Another illegitimate shortcut is summarizing a paragraph instead of providing a *full* translation. There is such a thing as summary translation of a paragraph or a document. If a summary is called for, then this is precisely what the translator is expected to provide. But the most common form of translation is what's known in the business as a verbatim translation, which is a full and complete rendition of the source text. When verbatim translation is ordered, anything less than a full translation is an illegitimate shortcut. Unfortunately, some translators tend to overlook this from time to time, especially when they undertake more work than they can accomplish by a given deadline, and decide to summarize rather than miss that deadline.

Perhaps the worst habit for a translator is to decide at a certain point in time that his or her knowledge of either the source or the target language is so good that it cannot possibly stand any improvement. The moment one stops growing linguistically, one is no longer on the cutting edge of one's profession. The good translator is a perennial language student, always eager and willing to learn more and to keep up with the latest.

As for good habits, the most important perhaps are the ones we obtain by reversing the above-mentioned bad habits. But there are many more. One excellent habit is to read professional literature in the field one will be called upon to translate with reasonable frequency. One good example is *Scientific American*, which can help anyone who translates subjects of science and technology to learn the style or styles used in scientific writing. People who work in the field of translating business documents should definitely read business periodicals, not the least of which is the *Wall Street Journal*. One does not have to be a scientist to translate scientific articles, or have a business degree to translate business documents, but a general understanding of the subject goes a long way in providing an accurate translation of the subject.

Another excellent habit is to translate not only for profit but also for enjoyment and for increasing one's experience. Most people, unfortunately, are not so taken with their daily work that they would want to continue doing it after hours for fun or practice. But an accomplished translator is someone who will on occasions translate simply for the sake of sharpening his or her skill, or accept a very small fee because of personal commitment to the subject matter, or because of a personal interest. This writer, for example, enjoys translating poetry because of the challenge of doing what is perhaps the most difficult type of translation, and, quite simply, because of the enjoyment of poetry.

Yet another good habit is to always be on the lookout for dictionaries. Many dictionaries are hard to find, and are available in few places. This writer in all his travels across the United States and abroad always stops in bookstores to look for dictionaries. One can also order dictionaries from bookstores and from publishers, but then one has to know what to order and from whom. (See Appendix 1).

The last good habit I would like to mention is the practice of compiling word lists and building a reference library.

Dictionaries do not have all the words and terms a translator needs, nor do they contain all the information which specialized references may have. There are aids for translators put out by certain organizations, and there is professional literature in every field. Good references are worth their weight in gold when they are needed for a specific translation.

Stories translators tell

Two new immigrants from the Far East meet on the street in Miami.

"I heard your nephew, who moved to Miami last year, is becoming Americanized very quickly."

"How so?"

"He speaks fluent Spanish."

José goes back to South America after a short stay in the States.

"The gringos are very nice people," he tells his friends. "I went to Yankee Stadium. There were no seats left, so they told me to stand by the flagpole. Suddenly everyone got up, turned to me, and sang in chorus: "José, can you see?"

6. TRANSLATION TECHNIQUES

Over time, translators develop personal techniques which enhance the quality and the speed of their translation. No one set of rules applies equally to everyone, but there are certain methods and means of translation which can help almost any translator achieve greater accuracy and output. The following is a review of some of the key techniques which are becoming almost universal among professional translators.

The first and foremost question a translator must deal with today is what kind of equipment to use in the process of translating. In the days of the pen and the typewriter this question was much less crucial. Today, however, translation has become almost totally dependent on computers, for several good reasons: (a) Word processing allows far greater flexibility in producing text than any other contemporary means. The output of most translators has been tripled and quadrupled through the use of computers. (b) Computers allow text to be stored on a disk and reprinted or modified later on, a function which is invaluable in the translation field. (c) Clients nowadays are getting used to asking for translation on disk, since it allows them to edit, reprint, modify and enhance the physical appearance of a document. (d) If more than one translator is involved in a given translation project, the text from the various translators can be entered by an editor on one disk and equalized or manipulated as necessary, without having to redo any particular portion thereof.

In addition, it is becoming more common every day to use electronic means such as a modem or a fax to transmit and receive text. These tools are no longer a luxury. The cost has been coming down, and more and more translators are acquiring them. Many people today are saying they cannot imagine how translators were ever able to manage without them. The answer is very simple: manage we did, but it took us ten days to two weeks to do what we can now receive, translate and deliver in two or three days.

The next question when approaching a translation assignment is: Am I qualified to do this particular translation? Only an honest answer will do. If one is not sure, then chances are one should not tackle that particular task. One must feel confident about a particular assignment if the results are to be satisfactory. The exception to this rule is a case where a client cannot find anyone else to do that particular job, and for some good reason is either willing to take a chance or to receive less than a complete and fully accurate rendition. In such a case it should be made clear between translator and client that the translation is not legally binding.

Once the commitment is made to proceed with the job, the translator will spend some time going over the entire document - even if it is book-length - and do a realistic assessment of the following points:

a. How long will it take to translate the document?
b. What reference tools are needed to get it done?
c. What kind of preliminary steps are needed prior to the actual work of translating?
d. What special problems are related to the document, such as legibility of blurred or poorly copied text or difficult handwriting?
e. Does the document contain text in a language or languages other than the main source language, and, if so, can the translator handle that language?

Regarding the question of time, one can do a quick estimate of the length of the document by averaging words per line, times lines per page, times number of pages. An experienced translator has a pretty good idea of the number of words per hour he or she can translate. This is an essential feature of undertaking a professional translation job, since most clients have tight deadlines and tend to give repeat business to those translators known for keeping their deadlines.

As for reference tools, if, for example, one is given a document about telecommunications, one should make use of one's own resources in that field and/or borrow from other sources whatever one needs to accomplish the task.

Preliminary steps prior to actual translation can include a consultation with an expert in a specialized technical field regarding a difficult term, phrase, paragraph or concept which the translator does not feel comfortable with. Having access to such experts is one of the translator's most cherished assets. It can make all the difference in the world between a correct and effective translation and one that simply misses the main point of the entire text. Another preliminary step is a trip to the local, regional or even specialized library to do some research on the subject.

The problem of legibility should be identified *before* one begins the task, not after. Sometimes the problem may start in the middle of the document and be so severe as to render the translation of the first part useless. In that case, the translator may have wasted a great deal of time. Sometimes the problem is minor, and does not affect the overall outcome of the translation. In other cases, the client may decide to proceed with the translation and simply put the designation [illegible] (between brackets rather than parentheses) wherever a word or part of the text cannot be deciphered.

Unbeknownst to client and translator, when a translation job is first assigned, there may be portions of text inside the source document in a language other than the main language of the document. This can happen in commercial, scientific and scholarly documents. It even happens in Tolstoy's novel *War and Peace,* when the author starts using French instead of Russian. This too should be detected prior to commencing the translation work, and a decision has to be made as to: (a) Does that text need to be translated? (b) Can the translator handle it? (c) Is it necessary to assign it to another translator?

Once all this preliminary work has been done, one is ready to proceed with the actual translation work.

Depending on the particular text, one should either start translating at this point, or, in the case of a text containing highly specialized terminology which may send the translator on frequent trips to the dictionary, one should first go through the document and make a list of as many unknown or uncertain terms as possible, and then spend some time looking them up and making a word list. This technique saves a great deal of time, since once a list is completed it is much easier to sail through the text, and the time spent initially on making the list is very short compared to the time wasted on repeated interruptions to look up words. Moreover, by first mastering the more difficult terminology of the text, one gains a much better understanding of the subject and is certain to produce a better translation.

Once the translation process is begun, one should follow good work habits. Some translators, particularly those engaged in freelance work, tend to overdo it, especially during their "busy season," when they can generate a large income during a relatively short period of time. They will go for twelve or more hours a day, and before they know it they will start complaining of stiffness in the neck and shoulders, blurred vision, and fatigue. One should not translate more than eight hours a day. Six is ideal. Eight is tolerable, provided one takes a few short ten to fifteen minute breaks. Ten is pushing it. Over ten is definitely hazardous to your health.

As was already explained, your personal computer is your best friend when it comes to translating, editing, and producing a final copy. One can learn a few basic commands, say, in WordPerfect, and start using the computer. But there is much more to the software than entering, deleting and inserting text. The better acquainted with the software you become, the more it will help you with translation. Learn how to do columns and tables, how to use special technical and scientific symbols, do graphic functions, use the spell-check and the thesaurus, create data bases for glossaries and for your own administrative records, and you will tackle a great variety of technical text in many fields at a speed that will amaze you. Remember: speed in translation is the most important thing next to language proficiency. Without it you will not be profitable, and you will be overrun by the competition. With an established record of fast accurate translation you can write your own ticket.

After a few years of using the computer you may want to consider dictation. Personally, I prefer a mix of PC and dictation. When I have an unusually long job and not enough time to do it in, I may revert to dictation. Otherwise, I prefer to word-process. One could argue that by dictating one gets more done and earns more, but there are other things to consider, such as the cost of transcription, the need to edit transcription, and the better control one has over writing than speaking. Some of us are natural speakers, others are writers.

One continues to develop translation techniques as time goes on. One of the most wonderful things about translation, in my opinion, is the fact that your mind is never idle, never in a rut, but rather always being challenged by new tasks, new subjects, new knowledge, and the need to keep up with new developments in language, with different fields of human knowledge, and with the events of the world. As a translator in the Washington area since the late seventies, I have found myself in the middle of world events, beginning with the peace treaty between Egypt and Israel in 1979, when I met Begin, Sadat and Carter, and, most recently, my daily dealings with events in post-Cold War Eastern Europe, with a strife-torn Middle East, the famine in Somalia, the new Free Trade Agreement between the United States and Mexico, and much more. Very few people and very few professions cover as broad an area as a translator. Every day we in the translation business find new challenges, and have to solve new problems. As a result, we are always developing new techniques and finding new answers.

7. TRANSLATION EQUIPMENT

There are certain tools translators today cannot do without. The first on the list is the computer. The computer most commonly used today by translators is the IBM or IBM-compatible PC, with the Macintosh coming a distant second. The Mac is better suited for graphics and desk-top publishing, while the IBM is still the king of word-processors. A translator's computer needs to be compatible with clients and with other translators if the work is to be acceptable. Otherwise, one will have to go through the difficult process of file conversion and a great deal of additional reformatting.

If you cannot afford a new computer, we suggest you start with a used one. Look for one in your local newspaper, and make sure you get one in good condition. If you look for a new computer, ask yourself whether you'd rather have a desktop PC or a notebook model (formerly called laptop). A good notebook computer is not more expensive than a PC, and it gives you incredible versatility. Ideally, you should have one of each, or at least a PC monitor - preferably a color one - you can hook up to your notebook when you compute at home, to gain the advantage of a larger, easier to use screen.

In selecting a computer, my first choice would be one of the new 486-33 MHz notebook or PC computers with at least 8 meg of RAM (memory), a hard-drive with a minimum of 250 meg, a good color monitor (your eyes are very important and worth preserving), and an internal fax-modem card. For the best price, shop around and compare prices. Special deals these days range between $1,500 and $2,000.

Your computer will come loaded with both DOS and Windows, the two basic operating systems for your word-processing software. For translation purposes, DOS suffices. The trend, however, is clearly towards Windows, so you may want to try Windows (using such an operating device as a mouse) as well.

There are, of course, higher capacity computers, which can give you more speed and more storage capability. It is only a question of how much you can and are willing to spend. You can get a computer with a CD-ROM (compact disc-read-only-memory) drive, and greatly increase your storage capacity, for such items as electronic dictionaries. When it comes to computers, the possibilities are unlimited.

The word-processing software most commonly used by translators is WordPerfect in either the 5.1, 6.0, or 6.1 version. Next comes Microsoft Word, which is becoming increasingly popular as a program used with Windows.

Modems, which transmit computer files over phone lines, come in different baud sizes (affecting volume and speed). I recall not so long ago a size of a few hundred baud. These days the popular size is 14,400 baud, but they go even higher.

Your internal fax is of limited use, since it does not handle hard copy. For regular flow of freelance translation, you may need a separate fax machine. Those have been coming down in price significantly, and you can now get a plain paper fax machine for a little over $300.

For doing word-processing in languages other than English, I recommend the WordPerfect foreign language modules. Those cover such European languages as Russian, Spanish, French, German, Italian and Portuguese, and non-European alphabet languages such as Arabic and Hebrew.

For Russian we also recommend Microsoft Word with the Exceller Russian package. Be sure you get a language module with the same version as your English version (5.1, 6.0 and so on).

For Chinese and Japanese there are several programs. Microsoft Word (2.0 and 6.0) is very good for Chinese text formatting, while Xialibaren (XLBR) is equally good for Chinese word-processing. For Japanese, WordPerfect sells a Japanese version in Japan.

25

Printers have also come down in price. The standard now is either laser or laser-quality. The size and quality of your printer will depend on the volume you produce. You can start with a small, inexpensive printer that prints a few pages per minute, and later upgrade to a higher capacity one.

Another great tool for translators is the optical scanner, which enables you to transfer text from a page to your computer (using the OCR - optical character reader), so that you can work on it as a regular file in WordPerfect or some other program. A scanner is also very useful for transferring charts and other graphic material from the original text into your translation text. A very good scanner is the HP ScanJet. A scanner is not a must for the beginning translator, but after you have done professional translation for a while you may want to consider getting one.

The power of language:

Once, in the "good old days," the Russian Czar decided to grant clemency to one of his unfortunate subjects who had been sentenced to death. He ordered his communications expert to send a telegram to the prison in Siberia, stating:

Clemency, period, no execution.

The careless clerk at the telegraph office did not proofread the telegram. It came out as:

Clemency no, period, execution.

---

8. DICTIONARIES AND REFERENCE LITERATURE

No translator, no matter how accomplished or well versed in both the source and the target languages, can do without dictionaries and reference literature. If either language or knowledge were static, remaining the same over a long period of time, then one could conceivably reach a level of expertise where references become marginal. The fact remains that this is not the case, certainly not in our day and age, when both language and knowledge are changing almost daily. If, for instance, you specialize in translating medical subjects, and you stop doing it for a few months, you may find out that there are new names of drugs, medical concepts and procedures which did not exist at the time you stopped translating. Therefore, you need current reference sources that will enable you to handle current medical subjects.

By the same token, the best of dictionaries and reference sources become dated the day they are published, and will never answer all your questions. This guide - for that matter - will have to be revised within at least a year from now, preferably sooner, if it is to keep up with all the information it seeks to provide (a supplement, in the form of a newsletter, will be provided on a semiannual basis for this purpose). In a sense, dictionaries and reference literature today are comparable to the phone book, which is reissued every year. What all this means to you as a translator is that even if you possess the best of linguistic and technical references, as indeed you should, you may want to get in the habit of compiling your own glossaries and databases in subjects you frequently translate, to keep yourself up to date, and always be on the lookout for new reference sources.

When you start out in this business, you soon discover that the acquisition of good dictionaries and reference literature is quite an expensive proposition. The best general and technical dictionaries in such major languages as Spanish, German, French and Japanese range in price from \$100 to over \$300 each. Good technical reference books in specialized subjects are not much cheaper. As a beginner, you may not be independently wealthy, and you may get an assignment which would require a couple of expensive dictionaries, but the money you earn from this assignment will not cover the cost of the dictionaries. What are you to do?

What I did when I started out some years ago as a freelance translator of Spanish and Hebrew, was to go to my regional public library, where they had some of the reference sources I needed. It was not as convenient as having your own, but it worked. Then, as I started earning more money from translation, I gradually acquired the dictionaries I needed. I must confess, sometimes I overindulged myself, and sometimes I bought dictionaries which weren't so good, and which I should have checked out more carefully. But my general policy has been to stay within my budget, and the times when I was able to acquire some of my best and most expensive reference sources was when I got an assignment in one of my languages of expertise big enough to justify the expense.

As of this writing, there is a growing trend in the publishing world to produce dictionaries and references on electronic media, such as computer disk, CD-ROM, and so on. If fact, books in general are moving away from "hard copy" to software. Does this mean we should stop buying dictionaries? I think not. Books are not going to disappear in the next few years, if ever. Typically, a professional translator engaged in a highly technical translation job will be surrounded by dictionaries and reference sources, spread out all over the table, or even covering the floor, looking up things in as many as ten or twelve different books at the same time. To do all of this on computer would necessitate either a ten or twelve-part split screen, with a great deal of key-punching or mouse-clicking, which may be more time consuming than simply having the good old books spread around you. Some day all of this may be overtaken by technology, but for the time being let's stick with books.

For recommendations of good dictionaries and reference sources, See Appendix 1. For major dictionary outlets, see Appendix 2.

Some uncomplimentary statements about translators:

It is difficult in following lines laid down by others not sometimes to diverge from them, and it is hard to preserve in a translation the charm of expressions. (St. Jerome)

Traduttori, traditori (translators are traitors). A traditional Italian statement.

Some hold translations not unlike to be
The wrong side of a Turkey tapestry. (James Howell)

Les traductions augmentent les fautes d'un ouvrage et en gâtet les beautés (Translations increase the faults of a work and spoil its beauties) (Voltaire)

Reading poetry in translation is like kissing a woman through a handkerchief (H. N. Bialik)

Nor ought a genius less than his that writ attempt translation (Sir John Denham)

---

9.   HOW TO OPERATE AS A FREELANCE TRANSLATOR

So you decided to try your hand at freelance translation. Congratulations! If this is indeed your calling, or your Karma, or your destiny, or whatever you choose to call it (as a translator you will always be compelled to choose the right word), stick to it, and your reward will be more than tangible. While not everyone may appreciate your work, since translation is - and has always been - one of the most misunderstood (sometimes even maligned) professions, if you maintain your professional integrity, you will always know your own self-worth, and your reputation will grow.

But getting down to reality. There are many mundane technical details one must master if one is to operate successfully as a freelance translator. Here are some of the most important ones.

Budgeting Yourself

Bear in mind that a freelancer has no job security, no steady biweekly or monthly paycheck, no tenure. You are in business for yourself, as a consultant, or a contractor, or a subcontractor. As such, you will experience periods of either feast or famine, and you will have to learn how to handle both.

I once knew a translator who did a large job, earned a few thousand dollars in less than two months, and spent the entire sum on an expensive notebook computer with a high-resolution color monitor, built-in fax, modem, and extra memory chips. Soon he ran into a long dry spell, and he needed the money to pay his bills. He had to sell his super-duper gadget at a considerable loss. He learned his lesson the hard way. He could have made do with a notebook half as expensive, and kept at least two thousand dollars in the bank. This would have carried him through the dry spell, until things started to pick up again (which they did). I believe he is now operating more prudently, and doing quite well.

It seems all freelancers learn this lesson at some point. Like a squirrel, we stash away some of our acorns for a rainy day. We learn how to look farther down our professional road, and by the time we have to sit down and do our tax return we feel a sense of satisfaction knowing we have provided well for ourselves, and have put aside enough to pay Uncle Sam.

Pricing Yourself

The next lesson we learn is that not all translation jobs were created equal. By that I mean, like a good businessperson, you learn how to price each job, and either accept it or reject it. I have dealt with many freelance translators in many different languages who decide beforehand that - like a lawyer at a high power law firm - they will not offer their services for less than, say, a hundred dollars an hour or twenty cents per word. Now, granted, there are a few translation and interpretation jobs around that will pay these high rates. But they are few and far between. I may be moving in the wrong circles, but quite frankly, while I have seen such rates being paid, they were quite exceptional, and I personally don't know any freelance translator who gets them on a regular basis.

The name of the game is earning money on a steady basis, not once in a blue moon. And to do so, one has to be flexible. Many a time I agreed to do a translation job for a client for less than it was worth, but my payoff often came when, soon thereafter, the same client, valuing the quality of my work and my near-fanatic adherence to deadlines, came back to me with another, often urgent job, and this time I charged a higher rate, which made up for the shortfall the first time around. In short, you quickly learn in this business that your potential clients - be they small or large companies, government agencies, academic institutions, it makes no difference who - are almost always looking for a bargain. While they may not argue with their

31

doctor or lawyer or even plumber about their rates, you can rest assured they will argue with you, and will always try at least one or two of your competitors, hoping to get a better rate. You have to be prepared to do "creative rate structuring" if you are to get that coveted job.

How do you know how much to charge for your services? There is no easy answer to this question, as any professional translator knows. A lot depends on who your clients are. As a general rule, for-profit organizations will pay more than not-for-profit, or public and government agencies. The rule of thumb is supply and demand. If the client can get it cheaper, you may not get that job. You have to establish for yourself what one may call a realistic rate. Don't go too high, but don't sell yourself too short.

To begin with, written translation work is normally charged by the word. I have known good fast translators to earn a good living at 3 or 4 cents per word (time is the real measure of your translation earning. The more words per hour you can translate accurately, the more you will earn). Many translators will be shocked to hear this. They will call these rates "slave wages," and refuse to talk to me again. These days the range of 7 to 10 cents per word for translation from a foreign language into English, and 8 to 12 cents per words for translation from English into a foreign language is considered normal. In California the rates are usually somewhat higher than on the East Coast, but then again, they pay more taxes over there. Rates have been changing in recent years, and will continue to change.

One way to find out what the going rate is, is by consulting the American Translators Association chapter in your community or region. Another is by talking to other translators. And, in addition, you learn by trial and error. After trying different rates, you will find out what your clients are comfortable with, and stick to those rates.

To reiterate: Try to charge your better paying clients more, and those less capable of paying, less. Always look at the greater picture of your total yearly earnings, rather than getting yourself hung up on each case, giving the client and yourself a hard time. Flexibility is the secret weapon of the freelancer.

Getting Paid

One more thing about payment. Since most people do not have a good understanding of what translation is all about, and that includes some of the largest corporations and law firms in the country, they may decide after you perform your translation that your work is not up to snuff, and they would either withhold payment or try to reduce it. If indeed you did a less than acceptable job, well, then, you have to bite the bullet and take a reduction in pay. But that often is not the case, and you can find yourself in a lurch. If you know and trust your client (you have worked with them before, or they are a very reputable entity in your community, etc.), then you just go ahead and do the work. But if you have the slightest doubt about getting paid, get something in writing from your client, such as a purchase order, or have the client sign a statement issued by you, stating your own terms, or even try to get some money down. Remember, you are now in business, not in a social or academic situation, and the business world is tough.

Equally important is keeping good records of your clients, and keeping notes on them, for two main reasons: First, you want to know a year or two from now if you had a problem with a client, so that you can act accordingly and not make the same mistake twice. Second, you want to keep in touch with your clients, letting them know you moved, or your phone number changed, or even drop them a card for the Holiday Season. Your goal is repeat business, which means steady income, and also validates your worth as a good translator.

There is a great deal more a freelancer needs to learn, mostly through trial and error. There is only so much a guide like this can teach. The rest is up to you.

10. WHERE TO FIND WORK

If you choose freelance translation, you should consider yourself a one-person translation company. Your main concern will be where to find work. The need for freelance translation is greater than anyone can estimate, and is clearly growing at a rapid rate. World-wide, translation is a multi-billion dollar industry. But finding translation work on your own is easier said than done. The main problem is that translation is hardly ever a steady, ongoing function of any particular work source, such as an embassy, a company, a government agency, or even a publisher. None of those needs translation every day of the year. Each of them may need a great deal of translation all at once (more than any one person can handle within the given time-frame), and then none for a long time. And, if any one of them needs translation on an ongoing basis, chances are a decision will be made to hire an in-house translator, rather than farm out the work.

The fact remains, however, that a well-rounded freelancer can earn well over $50,000 a year, and, in the case of highly specialized technical translators in major languages like Spanish, German, Japanese or Russian, even $100,000 or more. The secret to all of this is establishing for yourself a good clientele. There are two ways of doing it. The first and by far the hardest is finding your own clients and working with them directly. You may want to contact embassies, law firms, publishers, government agencies and so on, and solicit work directly from them. If you are fortunate enough to find some good steady clients on your own, you will be doing quite well. But the problem often lies in the word "steady." What seems to be a steady client today, may not be so steady tomorrow.

This brings us to the second, and by far the safer option, which is translation agencies. There are hundreds of those in the United States, and they handle millions of dollars worth of translation business every year. In this chapter we will discuss translation agencies, as well as direct sources of translation available to the freelancer.

Translation Agencies

Translation agencies, also known as translation companies, or translation bureaus, are for the most part privately owned commercial establishments ranging in size from one or two employees to ten or more, but hardly ever larger than ten. Some are divisions of larger companies, such as Berlitz, which is primarily a language school and publisher, offering translation as a secondary function. Some specialize in one language only, such as Spanish, German, or Japanese. Most offer several languages, and quite a few bill themselves as offering "all languages." This last type is somewhat pretentious, since there are more languages in the world than any one person can identify. But what they really mean is that they will make the effort to find a translator in almost any language they may be called upon to translate.

As a general rule, translation agencies employ relatively few in-house translators, since the flow of work in any given language is usually uneven. Instead, they rely on the services of a network of hundreds of freelancers who can handle a great variety of subjects. Those freelancers are located all over the United States and even abroad. The ones who are most reliable and professional get the major share of the work, and some of them earn the above-quoted figures.

As a freelancer, you need to cultivate at least one such agency, preferably two or three. The problem in working with only one is that, with few exceptions, there may not be a steady flow of work coming out of any given agency in any given language, in subjects you are equipped to handle. Two or three will give you better coverage, and assure a better flow. On the other hand, you may find yourself in a situation where all three ask you to do something at the same time, and you may not be able to do it. You need to establish an understanding with your agencies that would make an allowance for such a scenario, so that you don't spoil your relationship with any one of them.

The worst thing you can do as a freelancer working with translation agencies is overcommitting yourself. Your most important personal asset is your reliability. Once you fail to meet deadlines (keep in mind - the agency stands to lose a client if deadlines are not met), your reliability becomes questionable, and if you do it once too often, you may soon find out that those phone calls from the agency offering you work assignments stop coming.

Where do you look for translation agencies? Appendix 3 offers a listing of hundreds of such agencies. You can find more in the Yellow Pages, or through the ATA (American Translators Association), which has local chapters around the country. My suggestion is to start with those close to home (in this day and age of international electronic communications, distance has little meaning. But then again, close to home still works, because you can meet the people there, befriend them, and in some instances even avail yourself of their dictionaries and other resources.

Keep in mind that a translation company has overhead, and also needs to make some profit to stay in business. They do the hard work of finding translation assignments, and therefore share with you the profit from the job. You can usually make more money by going directly to the client, and if you have enough of your own clients you don't need the middlemanship of the translation company. But most freelance translators do need those companies, which invariably provide a more steady flow of work than what a freelancer can get on his or her own.

The two things all translation companies appreciate and reward in a freelancer are honesty and loyalty. If you agree to a deadline, stick to it. Don't renege on it at the last minute. That's a sure prescription to spoil your association with your company. Equally important is not to go behind the company's back and try to solicit its own clients directly. Some companies will make you sign an agreement to this effect. Other will rely on the honor system. Don't abuse their trust. It usually doesn't pay off.

Direct Sources of Work

Working with translation agencies does not stop you from finding your own clients, as long as there is no conflict of interest with the agency's clients. It would be impossible to list here all the potential sources of direct translation work, since they include practically the entire human race (everyone needs a personal document translated at some point). But there are some major sources which ought to be mentioned, and here are some of the more important ones.

a. Law Firms

Law firms are a major source of translation work. Some of the larger firms hire full-time translators or staff members who are bilingual, especially if they do business on a regular basis with a foreign entity. Most firms use translators on an as-needed basis. Legal translation is a specialized field where one should acquire experience working with legal documents. There are several legal specialties, such as patent law, international law, immigration, and so on. Each specialty has its own style and terminology, which a translator needs to become acquainted with. As a freelancer, adding legal translation to your list of specialties is an excellent idea. You will find out that your volume of translation will increase considerably by doing so.

b. International Corporations

Corporations doing business in other countries have to deal with documents originated in the languages of those countries or English documents that need to be translated into those languages. Here again we find the two approaches, of either hiring translators or farming out work to freelancers and to translation services. This field is perhaps the fastest growing source of translation in the closing years of the twentieth century. More and more major American companies are turning to international business as a way to offset the decline of business at home and to gain a share of the world market. Their need for translation is growing every day, and even those who have in-house translators are finding themselves using freelancers because of their volume of translation work.

If you are fortunate enough to form a relationship with a major company doing business overseas, you may find yourself in the enviable position of dealing with a major source of translation.

c.   Government Agencies

Government at all levels, from the municipal to the federal, needs translation. At the local level we find more and more city and county governments translating their pamphlets, brochures and other documents into the languages of their immigrant population, notably Asian languages and Spanish. At the federal level we find that although most translation work is contracted out to translation agencies, there is also work available for freelancers. One U.S. government agency, namely, JPRS (Joint Publications and Research Service), associated with the CIA, has been known to use hundreds of translators over the years. Since the end of the Cold War this major flow of translation work has subsided, but it is still worth looking into.

d.   Embassies and Consulates

These are not easy to penetrate, since they are foreign political entities and are always wary of the outside world. But there are certainly times when they need the services of local freelancers, and are worth trying, particularly if you have some personal contact in one of them.

e.   Publishers

Book publishers use freelance translators in many different ways. This is not an easy field to break into, particularly for the beginner. Many publishers turn to academia for translators, and if you are in academia and can translate from or into another language in your field of expertise, there is a chance you can get the work.   Others turn to established translators with name recognition. But it is certainly worth trying to query publishers and find out if they need your services.

f.   Networking

An excellent source of work for freelance translators is personal contacts with other translators.   The ATA's local chapters is one place where translators meet and get to know each other. The annual conference of the ATA holds a networking session, which is very valuable. One also meets translators through personal contacts in the translation field. Keeping in touch with other translators is a prime means of finding out about work sources and assignments.   There are clearly many advantages to networking in the translation field, and the more contacts one has the better.

11. SEEKING A TRANSLATION CAREER

Translators are not as visible to the general public as dentists or policemen, and therefore seem to be a rare breed. The fact is, thousands of translators work full-time in the U.S. Armed Forces, U.S. Government agencies, international corporations and organizations, law firms, medical organizations, and many more. I happen to know a large number of those translation professionals. Many of them seem to be quite happy and fulfilled in their career, and are paid respectable though not outrageous salaries.

If you consider pursuing translation as a full-time career, there are several things to consider, and here are some:

Level of Expertise

Besides being very proficient in both your source and target language, and having a good writing ability, you have to have expertise in the field you will be working in on a full-time basis. If, for instance, you become a full-time translator for the National Geographic Society, you will need a good background in geography, preferably a graduate degree in that field. Keep this in mind when you apply for an opening for a translator position in any given organization. Chances are they are looking for someone with a strong background in their field.

Translation Training

They will also be interested in your credentials as a professional translator. They may look for either a translation degree from an accredited institution, or for a certification from an organization such as the ATA, or, in the case of U.S. Government employment, for State Department certification. For courses and programs for translators in colleges and universities, and for ATA and State Department certification, see Appendix 4.

I am not trying to imply that you cannot find full-time employment as a translator without the above training or accreditation. Unlike medicine or law, translation is not a fully regulated profession by any means. While the above are very helpful, they are not a must. You can find employment as a translator on your own personal merit, provided you can prove that you have an exceptional ability to translate and a thorough familiarity with your subject. Many a career translator started out in a totally different field, and somehow by virtue of his or her special skills in this field became recognized as a reliable and much needed translator. This, of course, is up to you to figure out about yourself.

The Right Language

If your language of expertise is Maltese (the language of the Island of Malta), your chances of finding full-time employment as a translator in the United States are very slim. In all my years as a translation agency manager, I only had one request for Maltese (it came from the FBI, and they later changed their mind about doing it). I did find one person in the U.S. who could translate Maltese, but as I expected it was not his full-time occupation.

Invariably, a full-time translation career is possible if you work in one of the major languages of the world, such as Russian, Spanish, German, French, Italian, Portuguese, Japanese, Chinese, or Arabic.

Multiple Languages

If you are fortunate enough to be fluent in several languages, particularly major ones, you may want to consider a full-time translation career. Many organizations look for individuals like yourself, not the least of which are international companies, law firms, government agencies, and the United Nations.

Pros and Cons

A full-time translation job means steady income, benefits, and everything else that goes with steady employment. But like all other jobs, it also has its drawbacks. Unlike the freelancer, you don't enjoy the same sense of freedom and flexibility. You become locked into one area and one subject, and at times you may find it quite repetitive and unchallenging. You are also part of an organization which, like all organizations, has its own politics which you may not always find to be to your liking. If you are fortunate enough to work for a congenial organization, you are lucky. But this is not always the case. Ultimately, the decision of which way to go is up to you.

Some tips on sending out resumes for translation jobs:

1. Proofread your resume ten times. In this business you cannot afford any typos in your resume.

2. Know your potential employers. Be sure you have the right qualifications for what they are looking for.

3. Stick to the point. Don't tell them you like tennis or hockey. They are too busy to be bothered with your personal life.

4. Capitalize on your experience, especially if it is relevant to what they are looking for.

5. Don't write a "threadbare" resume. Make it substantial, but only put in pertinent information.

6. Use good quality laser-type printing.

7. Don't make it too fancy, just dignified.

---

12. TRAINING PROGRAMS

Several institutions, including universities, U.S. Government agencies, and world bodies like the United Nations provide translation education and training. Yet translator education in the United States is not nearly as advanced as it is in some other parts of the world. In fact, most working translators in America today were trained, so to speak, on the job. I happen to be one of them. My own personal background includes five years of graduate school, but it was not in the field of translation (although in some ways related to it). I picked up translation on my own as a young teenager, as part of my life-long flirtation with writing. During the past fifteen years I have worked with literally hundreds of translators, and I have watched many of them grow and develop on the job, as I took part in providing them with professional tips and practical advice. This guide is part of my own effort to put all that experience into writing for the benefit of present and future translators and students of translation. So if you wonder whether you have to take a course or a pursue a study program in order to become a translator, the answer is - not necessarily. There are, however, advantages to such programs, and if you have the opportunity to pursue them, you certainly should.

One very effective approach to translator education is to choose a practical field of knowledge where there is a growing need for translation, such as telecommunications, and get a degree in that field, while working on either a translation degree on improving your language and writing skills. There is always a need for a highly specialized technical translator in such a field, and if you establish a reputation for yourself as an authority in that area, you may find yourself very much in demand.

Appendix 4 provides you with a list of translator education programs around the country. This list is far from exhaustive, and you should consult your local college or university on this matter, since this type of program has been proliferating in recent years. You may also suggest to your local county or other type of government to invite a local senior translator to give an adult education class in translation, which can certainly benefit the community.

Bad Translation

Some years ago the Cincinnati Reds got to the World Series. The next day the following sign appeared all over town:

Darn tootin' we rootin'!

A newspaper reporter from a foreign country was in town that day. He didn't quite know what to make of this sign, and since he was too proud of his English expertise, rather than ask one of the locals to interpret, he came up with his own interpretation. He reported the event to his newspaper in these words:

> Signs appeared yesterday all over Cincinnati, Ohio, saying: "Damn all those car horns! We are go-ing back to our roots, namely, to the horse and buggy!

---

13. ORAL INTERPRETATION

A field closely related to translation is oral interpretation. Many translators also engage in interpreting, and many professional interpreters are known to do text translation as well. The two terms - translation and interpretation - are often confused, despite the fact that they are two distinctive functions. This guide is primarily concerned with text translation, but a few words about oral interpretation are in order.

Interpreting is divided into two categories - consecutive and simultaneous. In the first case, the interpreter waits for the speaker to finish a statement, and then repeats it in the target language. In the second, the interpreter - usually seated in a sound proof booth and using earphones - repeats into a microphone what the speaker says almost at the same time, for the benefit of those who do not know the source language and need a translation into their own language. Consecutive interpreting, quite naturally, is easier and less demanding than simultaneous, and therefore pays less. It is used in court hearings, business meetings, and many other situations where a language is not shared by all present. Simultaneous interpretation is used primarily in international conferences, and its practitioners are often referred to as conference interpreters. Another form of oral interpretation is "sight translation," in which the interpreter is given a written text to translate orally on the spot.

Oral interpretation is best suited for those who are exceptionally articulate, are at ease in front of an audience, have public speaking experience, and can speak both languages, in case they have to ask the speaker for a clarification. In speaking, one does not usually get involved in the kinds of complicated technical text one encounters on the printed page. Most conversation is conducted in general language, with an occasional use of a technical term. The spoken vocabulary is not generally as intricate as the written one, therefore the skill of the interpreter is articulation rather than a vast vocabulary.

Interpreting requires a training different from written translation. I would encourage those who are interested in translation yet are more at ease speaking than writing to pursue interpreter training. To my knowledge, the professional field of interpreting is not nearly as vast as that of translation. But there are thousands of full and part time interpreters employed in the United States, mostly by the court system and by international bodies such as the United Nations, the World Bank, the International Monetary Fund, and various U.S. Government agencies, notably the U.S. Department of State. Interpreters get involved in some very interesting assignments, such as interpreting for heads of state and for such world events as the Olympic Games. They often get involved in travel, serving as escort interpreters who accompany foreign dignitaries on official visits to the United States. Clearly, one definite requirement for interpreters is a gregarious and pleasing personality, a good appearance, good manners, social savvy, and a good sense of humor.

14. MACHINE TRANSLATION

Many people today are saying that computers will soon replace translators. Most of those people are not translation experts. In fact, hardly any of them are. Some point to the fact that computers have already replaced typists and secretaries and reduced the work force of many companies. All this reminds me of a remark by George Bernard Shaw, according to which a monkey could write *Hamlet* if it managed to hit all the right keys on the typewriter. Very few translators can lay claim to creating literary works on the order of *Hamlet*, but lumping translators with typists and office support staff is missing the whole point of translation. As long as language continues to communicate more than the immediate literal meaning of words, as long as there are shades of meaning which keep changing all the time, as long as people have to make value judgments about the meaning and intent of a text, one will continue to need human translators to get the job done.

Certain limited language environments do allow for machine translation. One example is the Canadian weather bureau, which transmits weather reports in both English and French. The number of words involved in the daily weather report is very limited, and can be easily programmed into a computer for translation from one language into another. Another example are official forms which contain simple basic questions. An organization such as NATO can have forms put out in ten different languages and set up a program to automatically translate each form into those languages. But when it comes to any substantial text, machine-translated documents always require the kind of editing which invariably takes more time than having the document translated by a human translator.

At the present time the ones who benefit the most from machine translation are not those who buy such services, but rather the companies who develop and manufacture the software and the translators who work on those machine translation projects either as developers of the programs or editors of the machine translated text. In other words, machine translation has not made translation cheaper for the average consumer of translation services, and therefore does not pose a threat to translators. There will always be a need for truly accomplished translators.

Example of machine translation from Russian into English:

Raw machine translation: A contemporary airport is the involved complex of engineer constructions and techniques, for arrangement of which the territory, measured sometimes is required by thousands of hectares (for example the Moscow Airport Domodedovo, Kennedy's new York airport.

Text edited by humans: The modern airport is an elaborate complex of engineering structures and technical devices requiring a large territory, which, in some places, measures thousands of hectares (for instance, Domodedovo Airport in Moscow or Kennedy Airport in New York).

---

15. TRANSLATION: A LIFE-LONG CAREER

The best thing about translation is that it is an activity you can pursue at different times of your life, and you can continue doing it or pick it up again even after you retire from your regular job. This has never been more true than today, in the age of electronic communications. I wrote several parts of this guide on the plane from Washington to San Diego, on the beach in Puerto Rico, and in other places I have lost track of, thanks to my six-pound Compaq notebook and my two-pound laserjet printer, two small items which travel with me almost everywhere.

When I get up too early to go to the office, I do some translating. When I have some time to kill between engagements, I do some more. Translation has put me in touch with more areas of human knowledge and endeavor than almost any other career is capable of doing. At one time or another, a translator becomes part of almost anything. During ten years of providing translation for U.S. Government agencies, I started with the State Department, moved on to the Defense Department, and at one time or another interacted with almost every federal department and agency. I can think of few other careers more challenging and fascinating.

But best of all, a translator never stops learning. Language keeps changing, knowledge keeps increasing, and the professional translator stays on top of it all. Once you have developed good translation habits, you will enjoy the continuous activity of learning new words and terms, and being part of the latest advances in many areas of human knowledge. It is, indeed, a privileged position.

I hope you have enjoyed reading this guide as much as I have enjoyed writing it, and that you will benefit from translation as much as I have. If that is the case, then my reward will be great indeed. I have felt for many years that translators deserve a better break than they have been getting in our largely insular, monolingual society. Most translators I have known were and are hard working folk, decent and dedicated people, friendly and generous, and it has been a special privilege for me to be their colleague and friend, as well as teacher and provider of translation work. There is no doubt in my mind that ours is a profession that will become more and more prominent as the twenty-first century begins to unfold, and for several years now I have felt a sense of exhilaration knowing that I am part of one of the great adventures of our time.

APPENDIX 1.

DICTIONARIES AND REFERENCE LITERATURE

For a general discussion of dictionaries and reference literature, see Chapter 8.

Translators use hundreds, perhaps thousands of different dictionaries and reference books. It is not quite possible to list all of them, but there are dictionaries and reference books that stand out, and a fair number of those are listed here, with some short comments.

The listing is arranged as follows:

A. General references
B. General and specialized dictionaries in the following major languages:

Arabic
Chinese
French
German
Hebrew
Italian
Japanese
Portuguese
Russian
Spanish

A. GENERAL REFERENCES

American English Dictionaries

What is the best dictionary for American English? The answer, quite simply, is none. American English is long overdue for some truly comprehensive dictionary, not unlike the complete Oxford Dictionary of British English. In its absence, the following general American English dictionaries are recommended, in a descending order:

The Shorter Oxford Oxford: Clarendon Press 1993 *This new two-volume dictionary provides a great deal from the complete Oxford as well as American and other kinds of English.*
The Third Webster International Springfield, MA: 1969 *This is the traditional "major" American-English dictionary. Though dated, it's still good to have around.*
Other large dictionaries of this kind are offered by Random House, American Heritage and others, but do not improve on the above two. For a smaller, very useful dictionary (of which there are many), we recommend: **Webster's New World Dictionary** Guralnik, D., ed., New York: Simon & Schuster, many editions.

American English Reference Books

Most translations into English, particularly technical ones, require what's known as "good idiomatic English." There are general rules of what is considered good writing style and good usage. Here are some of the key books in this field:

The Elements of Style, W. Strunk & E.B. White, many editions *A classic and a must.*
Modern America Usage Follett, W., New York: Hill & Wang 1966 *Old but useful. Many good tips on those English words, phrases and terms which are often misused.*
Roget's Thesaurus Many editions *Beware of the thesaurus! It may be useful as an intermediate step in your search for the right word, but not as the final authority.*
Style Manual U.S. Government Printing Office, Washington, DC *A must for translators involved in U.S. Government translations. The Government has its own rules of American English usage, which should*

be adhered to in this type of work.

Additional references:

MLA's Line by Line Cook, Boston: Haughton Mifflin
The Handbook of Good English Johnson, F.O.F.
The Elements of Grammar Shertzer, New York: McMillan
The Elements of Editing Plotnik, New York: McMillan
Handbook of American Idioms & Idiomatic Usage W. & D. Regents
Colloquial English Collis, Regents

General Reference Books

This type of book is hard to recommend. The field is so vast it would fill a separate volume. Here are some handy ones:

Columbia Desk Encyclopedia Comes in different sizes, and can help you (not always) with names, dates and other bits of information.
Almanacs Many different kinds. Of limited use to translators.
Atlases too many to enumerate. One of the best new ones is the **Times Atlas of the World.**

Business/Finance/Insurance/Real Estate

Dictionary of Business Terms Friedman, J., New York: Barron's 1987
Dictionary of Finance and Investment Terms Downes, J., New York: Barron's 1987
Dictionary of Banking Terms Fitch, T., New York: Barron's 1990
Dictionary of Insurance Terms Rubin, H., New York: Barron's 1987
Dictionary of Real Estate Terms Friedman, J., New York: Barron's 1987

Chemical/Life Sciences

You can find multi-volume encyclopedias of chemistry in the public libraries that will answer many of your questions. But as your questions become more and more specific, you will need very specialized reference material in the many specialized areas of chemistry and life sciences, which are often published by government, public and private organizations, such as the World Health Organization, pharmaceutics companies, and many more.

Computers

Here the field changes almost daily. For some quick, handy sources on basic computer terminology, you may try:
Dictionary of Computer Terms Convington, M., New York: Barron 1992
Webster's New World Dictionary of Computer Terms New York: Simon & Schuster 1988
The Illustrated Computer Dictionary New York: Bantam Books 1988

Electric/Electronics

Standard Dictionary of Electrical and Electronic Terms Jay, F., ed., New York: Institute of Electric and Electronic Engineers 1992

Law

Black's Law Dictionary Black, H. C., St. Paul, MI: West Publishing 1991 *The standard book in its field.*
Law Dictionary Gifis, S., New York: Barron's 1984

Medical

The Bantam Medical Dictionary New York: Bantam 1982
Dictionary of Medical Terms Rothenberg, M., New York: Barron's 1989

Military

For all military materiel, the Jane series (annual, London: Jane's Publishing Co.) is the key source:

Jane's All the World's Aircraft
Jane's Fighting Ships
Jane's Weapon Systems
Also recommended:
Encyclopedia of the U.S. Military Arkin, W., New York: Harper & Row, 1990
The Dictionary of Modern Warfare Luttwak, E., New York: HarperCollins, 1991

Science and Technology General Reference

McGraw-Hill Dictionary of Scientific & Technical Terms Parker, S., New York: McGraw-Hill, 1994 *One of the finest one-volume references covering all science and technology. A must for any technical writer.*

ARABIC

General Dictionaries

A Dictionary of Modern Written Arabic, Wehr, H. Wiesbaden: Otto Harrassowitz 1979   *This is one of the best general Arabic-English dictionaries around. Available in hard cover and paperback.*
Dictionary of Egyptian Arabic Hinds, Martin, Beirut: Librairie du Liban 1987   *Egyptian terms.*
The Oxford English-Arabic Dictionary of Current Usage Doniach, N.S., Oxford: Oxford University Press 1972
Al-Fara'id al-Durriyah Hava, G., Beirut: Dar al-Mashriq 1982
An Arabic-English Lexicon, 8 vols., Lane, Edward W., Beirut: Librairie du Liban 1980
Arabic-English Lexicon, 2 vols., Lane, Edward W.,Cambridge: Islamic Texts Society 1984
As-Sabil: Dictionnaire Arabe-Francais/Francais-Arabe Reig, D. Paris: Librairie Larousse 1983
Dictionnaire des Sciences de la Nature, Ghaleb, E., Beirut: Imprimerie Catholique 1965

Arabic: Agriculture

Chihabi's Dictionary of Agriculture and Allied Terminology Al-Khatib, A. (ed.) 1978

Arabic: Botany

Illustrated Polyglot Dictionary of Plant Names Bedevian, A., Cairo: Argus and Papazian Presses 1936

Arabic: Business

The Office Dictionary in English and Arabic, Compiled by Multi-Lingual International Publishers Ltd, London: Oxford Univ. Press
English-Arabic Dictionary of Accounting and Finance Abdeen, A., Beirut: Librairie du Liban, John Wiley & Sons 1981

Arabic: Economics

Dictionnaire des Termes Economiques et Commerciaux Hinni, M., Beirut: Librairie du Liban 1972

Arabic: Geography

Dictionary of Arabic Topography and Place Names Groom, N., London: Librairie du Liban 1983

Arabic: Legal

Faruqi's Law Dictionary (Ar-Eng) Faruqi, H., Beirut: Librairie Liban 1972

Arabic: Military

Al-Mu'jam al-'Askari al-Muwahhad Committee for Standardizing Military terminology for Arab Armies.

Arabic: Science and Technology

A New Dictionary of Scientific and Technical Terms Al-Khatib, A., Beirut: Libraire du Liban 1971   English-Arabic

CHINESE

General Dictionaries

A Chinese-English Dictionary Compiled by Beijing Foreign Languages Institute, Chinese-English Dictionary Editorial Committee, Hong Kong: Commercial Press 1981   *A very good mid-sized dictionary. Entries are arranged alphabetically but there is also a character index.*
Xinhua Cidian Beijing: Commercial Press 1980   *The most basic reference. Indispensable.*
Chinese Idioms and Their English Equivalents Chen Yongzhen and Spring Chen, Hong Kong: Commercial Press 1983   *A must for anyone translating general Chinese text.*
Chinese Cihai Shanghai: Shanghai Cishu Chubanshe 1979   *The staple reference of Chinese translators for years.*
Handbook of Chinese-English Phrases Beijing: Waiwen Chubanshe 1970
A Dictionary of World Place Names Shanghai: Shanghai Cishu Chubanshe 1981
A New Practical Chinese-English Dictionary Liang Shih-ch'iu, ed., Taipei: The Far East Book Co 1975
The Shogakukan Dictionary of New Chinese Words Tokyo: Shogakukan 1985
Visual Dictionary Corbeil, J.C., ed., Hong Kong: Readers' Digest Association Far East Ltd. 1988
Xinhua Cidian Beijing: Commercial Press 1980
Chinese-English Dictionary of Contemporary Usage Wen-shun Chi, compiler, Berkeley: University of California Press 1977
Reverse Chinese-English Dictionary Beijing: Commercial Press 1985
A Classified and Illustrated Chinese-English Dictionary Hong Kong: Joint Publishing Company 1981

Chinese: Aerospace

English-Chinese Aviation Dictionary Hua Renjie, ed., Beijing: Shangwu Yinshuguan 1982

Chinese: Agriculture

A Chinese-English Dictionary of China's Rural Economy Kieran Broadbent, Farnham Royal, Bucks, England: Commonwealth Agricultural Bureau 1978

Chinese: Chemical

Chinese-English-Japanese Glossary of Chemical Terms Tokyo: Toho Shoten, Ltd 1977 *Far from complete, but there are very few other such sources available in this field. Entries are arranged by number of strokes in a character.*

Chinese: Civil Engineering

English-Chinese Dictionary of Civil and Architectural Engineering Terms Hong Kong: Commercial Press, 1979

Chinese: Computers

A Comprehensive IBM Computer Dictionary Science Popularization Press, 1985
English-Chinese Computer Dictionary Beijing: Renmin Youdian Chubanshe 1984
English-Chinese Computer Software Dictionary Zhou Hanzong, ed., Changsha: Hunan Kexue Jishu Chubanshe 1986

Chinese: Economics/Industry

English-Chinese Accounting Dictionary Beijing: Shiyou Gongye Chubanshe 1982 *Good, reputable reference.*
Nichi-Ei-Chu Boeki Yogo Jiten Eds., Shangwu Yinshuguan, Toho Shoten. Tokyo: Toho Shoten 1986
Chinese-English Dictionary of Economic Terms China Commercial Press 1988
Dictionary of International Trade and Finance Chung-hwa Cheng-hsin-swo Inc. Publishing Department Taipei, Taiwan: 1989
English-Chinese, Chinese-English Dictionary of Business Terms Chu Hsiu-feng, ed. Hong Kong: Chi Wen Publishing Co. 1973
New Chinese Dictionary of Economics and Trade Harbin Press, 1989
English-Chinese Dictionary of Highway Engineering Beijing: Renmin

Jiaotong Chubanshe 1978
English-Chinese Dictionary of Railway Terms Beijing: Renmin
Tiedao Chubanshe 1977
English-Chinese Economic Glossary Chongqing: Zhongguo Shehui
Kexue Chuabanshe 1983
An English-Chinese Glossary of International Finance and Trade
Beijing: Zhongguo Zhanwang Chubanshe 1984
An English-Chinese Lexicon of International Economy Beijing:
Zhongguo Shehui Kexue Chubanshe 1984
Glossary of Foreign Exchange Terms Caizheng Jingji CHubanshe
1980
A Chinese-English Textile Dictionary Zhu Zhengdu, Lou Erduan et
al. Beijing: Fangzhi Gongye Chubanshe 1985
A Dictionary of Economic Management Terms Changchun: Jilin
Renmin Chubanshe 1982
English-Chinese & Chinese-English Accounting Dictionary Ji Zehua,
ed. Hong Kong: Wan Li Book Co. 1964
**An English-Chinese Dictionary of Finance, Economics and
Accounting** Chen Jinchi, Beijing Economics Institute, Beijing:
Zhongguo Caizheng Jingji Chubanshe 1987
An English-Chinese Dictionary of Economics and Finance Hu Xisen,
Yu Jialai and Qu Wanfang, Beijing: Shiyou Gongye Chubanshe 1986

Chinese: Electric/Electronics

Chinese-English Dictionary of Electronics Technology Gan Dayon,
ed., Beijing: Dianzi Gongye Chubanshe 1987   *A valuable reference.*
English-Chinese Dictionary of Electrical Engineering Beijing: Kexue
Chubanshe 1987
English-Chinese Dictionary of Data Communications Technology
Electrical Engineering Press 1990
English-Chinese Dictionary of Remote Sensing Li Wenlan, ed.,
Beijing: Kexue Puju Chubanshe 1986
English-Chinese Dictionary of Television and Electronics Beijing:
Kexue Chubanshe 1987
English-Chinese Dictionary of Television and Video Recording
Beijing: Renmin Youdian Chubanshe 1983

Chinese: Fiber Optics

English-Chinese Lightwave Communications and Optical Fiber Technical Dictionary Li Guangqian, ed., Beijing: Renmin Youdian Chubanshe 1985

Chinese: Geology

Geology Dictionary Ministry of Geology and Mineral Resources, Beijing: Dizhi Chubanshe 1983
English-Chinese Comprehensive Geology Dictionary Beijing: Kexue Chubanshe 1980

Chinese: Laser/Infrared

English-Chinese Dictionary of Lasers and Infrared Technique Zhou Rongsheng, ed., Beijing: Kexue Chubanshe 1987

Chinese: Military

Cihai, Military Supplement Shanghai: Shanghai Cishu Chubanshe 1980   *A must, just as the "Cihai" itself.*
English-Chinese Military and Technical Dictionary Jiang Kang, Lu Zuokang, ed., Luoyang: Yuhang Chubanshe 1985

Chinese: Scientific/Technical

A Modern Scientific and Technical Dictionary Shanghai: Shanghai Scientific and Technical Publishing House 1980   *Highly recommended.*
Chinese-English Dictionary of Scientific and Technical Terms Harbin: Heilongjiang Renmin Chubanshe 1985   *One of the best, but unfortunately not available from the publisher.*
An English-Chinese Dictionary of Technology Edited by Qinghua University specialist group, Beijing: Guofang Gongye Chubanshe 1978 *Recommended.*
A Modern Science and Technology Dictionary Shanghai: Shanghai Kexue Jishu Chubanshe 1980

FRENCH

General Dictionaries

Harrap's New Standard French & English Dictionary, 4 vols., London: George G. Harmp & Co Ltd. 1981 *This is the best French-English English-French dictionary for all-around translation use, and arguably one of the finest examples of lexicography in any language. One can only wish this kind of a dictionary existed in every language.*
Collins-Robert French Dictionary New York: HarperCollins 1987 *Arguably the best one-volume French-English English-French all-around dictionary for translators.*
Lexis, Dictionnaire de la langue française, Larousse 1977
Dictionnaire usuel illustre, Flammarion 1983
Dictionnaire des neologismes officiels Fantapie, A., Franterm 1984 French-English, English-French.
Dictionnaire des expressions et locutions figurées Rey, A., Chantreau, Sophie Robert, Paris: 1979   French-French.
Le Petit Robert Robert, P., Paris: Robert 1982   French-French.
Petit Larousse Illustre Larousse 1987
Dictionnaire des Mots Contemporains Gilbert, P., Paris: Robert 1985
Dictionary of Modern Colloquial French Herail and Lovatt, London: Routledge 1984
The Oxford-Duden Pictorial French-English Dictionary Oxford: Clarendon Press 1983
Dictionnaire de l'argot Colin, J.P., Paris: Larousse 1990.
A Dictionary of Colorful French Slang and Colloquialisms Deak, Etienne and Simone, New York: Dutton 1961

French: Aerospace

Dictionnaire de teledetection aerospatiale, Paul, S., Paris: Masson 1982   French-English
Dictionnaire de l'aeronautique et de l'espace Goursau, Henri St. Orens-de Gameville 1986

French: Automotive

Glossary of Automotive Terminology Chrysler Corporation, Warrendale, Pennsylvania: SAE Publications   French-English,

English-French.

French: Chemistry

French-English Dictionary for Chemists, Patterson, Austin M.
New York: Wiley & Sons 1921

French: Computers

Dictionnaire d'informatique, bureautique, telematique Ginguay, M.
Paris: Masson
Dictionnaire informatique, Fisher, Renee, Eyrolles 1984
French-English, English-French.
Dictionnaire de la microinformatique Fantapie, Alain,
Paris: Franterm 1984   French-English.
Dictionnaire de l'informatique Morvan, Pierre, Paris: Librairie
Larousse 1981
Harrap's French and English Dictionary of Data Processing,
Camille, Claude, London: Harrap 1981

French: Economics

Delmas/Harrap Business Dictionary Delmas/Harrap, London: Harrap
& Co Ltd. 1979
Glossaire des communautés européennes Conseil des communautes
européennes 1980
Dictionnaire des affaires Peron, M., Paris: Librairie Larousse 1968
Dictionnaire de la comptabilité Sylvain, F., Toronto: Institut
Canadien des Comptables Agrees
Dictionary of Business: English-French, French-English Collin, P.H.,
Teddington, Middlesex: Peter Collin Publishing, Ltd. 1990

French: Electronics

International Electrotechnical Vocabulary, General Index Geneva:
International Electrotechnical Commission 1979

French: Legal

Dictionnaire juridique et économique Doucet, Michel Paris: La
Maison du Dictionnaire 1979

Dictionnaire juridique, Quemner, Th.A., Paris: Editions de Navarre 1977 French-English.

French: Medicine

Dictionnaire Français-Anglais/Anglais Français des termes médicaux et biologiques Lepine, P., Paris: Flammarion Medecine-Sciences 1974
Dictionnaire Anglais/Français des sciences médicales et paramédicales Delamare, J., Edisem, Inc. 1978
Dictionnaire de médecine Hamburger, Jean, Flammarion 1982

French: Military

Lexique militaire Ottawa, Canadian Forces Headquarters 1982
English-French, French-English.
Glossaire militaire Imprimerie Nationale 1982
English-French, French-English.

French: Political

Dictionnaire Français-Anglais-Anglais-Français Dubois, Marguerite M., Larousse

French: Technical

French Technical Dictionary London: Routledge 1994   French-English, English-French   *Very comprehensive.*
Dictionary of Engineering and Technology Ernst, Richard, Wiesbaden: Oscar Brandstetter Verlag 1982   French-English.
Dictionnaire international d'abreviations scientifiques et techniques Azzaretti, M., La Maison du Dictionnaire 1978

GERMAN

General Dictionaries

Langenscheidts Enzyklopädisches Wörterbuch (Der Grosse Muret-Sanders) 4 vols., Berlin: Langenscheidt 1989   *The best all-around German-English, English-German dictionary. Quite expensive ($135 per volume), but definitely a good investment for the German-English translator.*

Duden Wörterbuch der Abkürzungen von Werlin, Josef Mannheim: Dudenverlag 1987   *Recommended.*

Langenscheidts Grosswörterbuch   Messinger, Heinz, Berlin: Langenscheidt 1982

Collins German-Engish/English-German Dictionary William Collins Sons & Co Ltd. 1980

English-German/German-English Dictionary Wildhagen Heraucourt, Wiesbaden: Brandstetter Verlag 1972

Brockhaus-Wahrig-Deutsches Wörterbuch Brockhaus, F.A., Wiesbaden: 1980

The Oxford-Harrap Standard German-English Dictionary Jones, Trevor, ed., Oxford: Clarendon Press 1977

Duden Deutsches Universal Wörterbuch Mannheim: Dudenverlag 1983   German-German.

Deutsches Wörterbuch Wahrig, Gerhard, Gutersloh: Bertelsmann Lexikon-Verlag 1979   German-German.

Grosses Abkürzungsbuch Koblischke, Heinz, Leipzig: VEB Bibliographisches Institut Leipzig 1985

German: Chemistry

Chemie und chemische Technik Technische Universitat, Dresden: VEB Verlag Technik 1992   German-English. *Recommended.*

Dictionary of Chemistry & Chemical Engineering DeVries Verlag Chemie 1978   German-English.

German-English Dictionary for Chemists Patterson, A.M., New York: Wiley & Sons 1963

German: Computers

Wörterbuch der Datentechnik Brinkmann, Schmidt, Wiesbaden: Brandstetter Verlag 1989   German-English, English-German. *Recommended.*
Fachausdrücke der Text-und Datenverarbeitung, IBM Deutschland 1978   English-German.
Technik-Wörterbuch Mikroelektronik Bindmann, Berlin: VEB Verlag Technik   English-German, German-English.
Technische Kybernetik Junge, Berlin: VEB Verlag Technik 1982 English-German, German-English.
Fachwörterbuch Energie-und Automatisierungs Technik Siemens German-English.

German: Economic

Dictionary of Legal, Commerical and Political Terms Dietl, Moss & Lorenz, Verlag C.H. Beck 1992   German-English, English-German. *Recommended.*
Cambridge-Eichborn German Dictionary Cambridge: Eichborn/ Cambridge University Press 1983   German-English, English-German.
German-English Glossary of Financial and Economic Terms Gunston, C.A.; Comer, C.M., Frankfurt am Main: Knapp Verlag 1983
Wörterbuch der Rechts-und Wirtschaftssprache   Alfred Romain, Munich: Verlag C.H. Beck 1983
Business German Clarke, S., New York: HarperCollins 1992

German: Electronics

Elektrotechnik-Elektronik   Budig, Peter-Klaus, Berlin: VEB Verlag Technik 1982   German-English.
Dictionary of Microelectronics & Microcomputer Technology Attiyate & Shah, VDI Veriag 1984
Lexikon der Elektronik, Nachrichten und Elektrotechnik Wemicke, Harry Deisenhofen: Verlag H. Wernicke 1979   Ger-English-German.

German: Legal

Dictionary of Legal, Commerical and Political Terms Dietl, Moss & Lorenz, Verlag C.H. Beck 1992   German-English, English-German. *Recommended.*

German: Medicine

Medizinisches Wörterbuch Unseld, D., 1978
German-English, English-German.
Wörterbuch für Aertzte (Dictionary for Physicians) German-English.
Stuttgart: Georg Thieme Verlag
Wörterbuch der Medizin und Pharmazeutik Bunjes, Werner E.

German: Maritime

Schiffstechnisches Wörterbuch Dluhy, R., Vincentz Verlag 1983
English-German, German-English.
Schiffahrts Wörterbuch Hamburg: Horst Kammer German-English-French-Spanish-Italian.

German: Nuclear Energy

Engineering Freyberger, G.H. Thiemig Verlag 1979 English-German, German-English.
Wörterbuch der Kraftwerkstechnik Konventionelle Dampfkraftwerke, Kernkraftwerke, Stattmann, F., Thiemig Verlag 1971

German: Patents

Dictionary of Patent Practice Uxekull, J.-D., 1977 German-English, English-German.

German: Technical

Dictionary of Engineering and Technology Ernst, R., Wiesbaden: Brandstetter Verlag 1980 *Recommended.*
Anglo-American and German Abbreviations in Science and Technology Wennrich, P., New York: Bowker 1976-78
Solid-State Physics and Electronic Engineering Bindman, W. 1972 German-English, English-German.
The Compact Dictionary of Exact Science and Technology Kucem, A., Wiesbaden: Brandstetter Verlag 1982 English-German, German-English
The Oxford-Duden Pictorial German-English Dictionary New York: Oxford University Press 1984
German-English Technical & Engineering Dictionary De Vries

London: McGraw-Hill 1965

Kraftfahrzeugtechnisches Handbuch Wyhlidal, F. Sprachdienst GmbH, Leonberg, Germany

Fachwörterbuch Energie und Automatisierungstechnik Beznei Heinrich, Siemens Aktiengesellschaft 1985 German-English.

HEBREW

General Dictionaries

Milon Ivri Shalem Alkalai, R., Ramat Gan: Masada 1969   Hebrew-Hebrew, 3-vols. *A good authority on contemporary Hebrew.*

Otzar Hashafa Haivrit Stuchkov, N., New York: Schulsinger, 1968 *A major Hebrew thesaurus.*

Yad Halashon Avineri, Y., Tel Aviv: Izraeel, 1964 *A treasury of Hebrew elucidations.*

Konkordantzya LaTanakh Mandelkern, S., Tel Aviv: Schocken 1969 *The guide to finding every word and phrase in the Bible.*

A Dictionary of the Targumim, the Talmud Babli and Yerushalmi, and the Midrashic Literature Jastrow, M., New York: Pardes 1950 *The guide to classical Hebrew and Aramaic. Two volumes. Hebrew-English.*

The Comprehensive Hebrew Calendar Spier, A., New York: Behrman House, 1952   *The Hebrew and general calendars, 1900-2000.*

Milon Olami L'ivrit meduberet Ben-Amotz, D., Jerusalem: Levin-Epstein 1972   *An excellent source of Israeli slang.*

The Complete English-Hebrew Dictionary Alkalai, R., Tel Aviv: Masada several editions   Hebrew-English, English-Hebrew. *Good general source, somewhat dated.*

The Megiddo Modern Dictionary Sivan, R., Tel Aviv: Megiddo 1982 English-Hebrew, Hebrew-English. *Newer than the Alkalai, but not as good.*

Hebrew: Computers

Dictionary of Electronic and Computer Terms Bick, J., ed., Bnei Brak: Steimatzky, 1991   Hebrew-English, English-Hebrew

Hebrew: Economics

Milon Munakhim Yakir, A., Tel Aviv: Heshev, 1989   Hebrew-English

Hebrew: Legal

Legal Dictionary Shaked, E., Bnei Brak: Steimatzky, 1992
Legal Dictionary Moses, E., Tel Aviv: 17 Shprintzak St. 64738

Hebrew: Medical

Dictionary of Medical & Health Terminology Feingold, E.,
Jerusalem: Carta, 1991

Hebrew: Military

Lexicon Dvir, Munakhim Tzvaiim Burla, Y., Tel Aviv: Dvir, 1988

Hebrew: Technical

The Technical Dictionary Gafni, H., Jerusalem: Keter, 1977
Hebrew-English, English-Hebrew
Technical Dictionary Ettingen, S.G., Tel Aviv: Yavneh, 1972
Hebrew-English-French-German-Russian

ITALIAN

General Dictionaries

Sansoni-Harrap Italian-English/English-Italian, 4 vols., Macchi, Vladimiro, London: 1981   *Extensive, expensive.*
Prontuario dei termini politici, economici, sociali in uso in Italia Ferrau, Alessandro Rome: Zingarelli Editore S.p.A. 1974
Dizionario della lingua italiana Devoto, G., Florence: Le Monnier 1980   Italian-Italian.
Grande Dizionario Hazon Garzanti Garzanti Editore S.p.A. 1984 English-Italian, Italian-English
La nuova enciclopedia universale Garzanti 1982 Italian-Italian.
Collins/Sansoni Italian Dictionary Macchi, V., Glasgow/Florence: 1981   Italian-English, English-Italian.
Ragazzini Dizionario Zanichelli, Nicola, Bologna: **1967**
Il nuovo Zingarelli vocabolario della lingua italiana Zingarelli, N., Bologna: Nicola Zanichelli 1983   Italina-Italian

Italian: Economic

Nuovissimo dizionario Commerciale Ragazzini, G.; Gagliardelli, G., Milan: Mursia 1976   English-Italian, Italian-English.
Dictionary of Commerce (It-Eng/Eng-It), Motta, G. Milan: Carlo Signorelli Editore 1978   Italian-English, English-Italian.

Italian: Medical

Dizionario medico Lauricella, Emanuele, Florence: Sadea 1961 Italian-Italian

Italian Naval

Grande dizionario di marina Silorata, M.B. Cava dei Tirreni: Di Mauro 1970   English-Italian, Italian-English.

Italian Technical

McGraw-Hill Zanichelli Dizionario enciclopedico scientifico e tecnico Bologna: Nicola Zanichelli 1980   English-Italian, Italian-

English.

Dizionario tecnico Marolli,G., Florence: Le Monnier 1980
English-Italian, Italian-English.

Dizionario tecnico Denti, R., Milan: Ulrico Hoepli Editore 1981
Italian-English, English-Italian.

JAPANESE

General Dictionaries

Shin Waei Daijiten Masuda, Ko Tokyo: Kenkyusha 1981
Highly recommended. Includes many examples of usage.
Kojien Shinmaru, Izuru, Tokyo: Iwanami Shoten 1991
Seikai Kancho Jinjiroku Tokyo: Toyo Keizai Shinposha
Japanese Family Names in Chinese Characters - A Guide To Their Readings Nihon Seimei, Yomifuri Jiten Sei no Bu, Tokyo: Nichigai Associates 1990 *This or a similar name dictionary is a must.*
Nandoku Seishi Jiten Ono, Shiro; Fujita, Y., Tokyo: Tokyodo 1977
Nichibei Hyogen Jiten Iwazu, K., Tokyo: Shogakkan 1984
Iwanami Kokugo Jiten Nishio, M., Tokyo: Iwanami Shoten 1971
Nichibei Kogo Jiten Seidensticker, E., Tokyo: Asahi Shuppansha 1978
Nihon Chimei Hatsuon Jiten Nihon Hoso Kyokari, Tokyo: Nihon Hoso Shuppan Kyokai 1959
Shin Eiwa Daijiten Koine, Y., Tokyo: Kenkyusha 1983
Waei Honyaku Handbook Murata, S., Tokyo: The Japan Times, Ltd 1991
Shin Gijutsu Ryakugo Jiten Aoyama, K., Tokyo: Kogyo Chosakai Publishing Co. 1985

Japanese: Economic

Advanced Business English Dictionary, revised edition Kobayashi, H., Tokyo: Pacific Management Consultants, Global Management Group 10 Nov 1987
Nihon Shoko Keizai Dantai Meibo (The Economic & Industrial Organiztaions in Japan), Tokyo Chamber of Commerce and Industry 1982
Keizai Yogo Jiten Hasegawa, H., Tokyo: Fujishobo 1985
New Japanese-English Dictionary of Economic Terms Tokyo: The Oriental Economist 1985
Waei Keizai Eigo Jiten Hanada, M., Tokyo: The Japan Times, Ltd. 1976

Japanese: Technical

Kagaku Gijutsu 35-Mango Daijiten Tokyo: Interpress 1990   *A most comprehensive general purpose Japanese technical dictionary. A reliable source of scientific terms.*
Kagaku Daijiten, Tokyo: Maruzen 1985
Magurokiru Kagaku Gijutsu Yogo Daqiten McGraw-Hill Science and Technology Dictionary Tokyo: Nikkan Kogyo Shimbunsha 1982
Nikkei High-Tech Dictionary Tokyo: Nihon Keizai Shimbunsha 1983

PORTUGUESE

General Dictionaries

The New Michaelis Dictionaries Sao Paulo: Edicoes Melhoramentos 1992   *A series of dictionaries. The Novo Michaelis Portuguese-English, English-Portuguese is a good comprehensive dictionary.*
Novo Dicionario Aurelio da Lingua Portuguesa Aurelio Buarque de Holanda, Ferreira, J.E.M.M. Editories, Ltda. 1986   Portuguese-Portuguese.
Dicionario de Expressoes Idiomaticas Pugliesi, M., Editora Parma Ltda. 1981   Portuguese-Portuguese.
The New Appleton Dictionary of the English and Portuguese Languages Houaiss, A., New York: Appleton-Century-Crofts 1967
A Portuguese-English Dictionary Taylor, J., Stanform University Press 1984
A Dictionary of Informal Brazilian Portuguese Chamberlain, B., Washington, DC: Georgetown University Press 1983
The Translator's Handbook Pennsylvania State University Press 1984

Portuguese: Computers

Dicionario de Informatica Lisbon: Publicacoes Dom Quixote 1984
Dicionario de Informatica Society of Computer and Peripheral Equipment Users, Rio de Janeiro: 1985

Portuguese: Economic

Dicionario de Economia e Gestao Lima, G., Porto: Lello & Irmao, Editores 1984

Portuguese: Legal

Dicionario Juridico Port-Ing/Ing-Port Chavez, M., ed., Rio de Janeiro: Barrister's Editora 1987
Vocabulario Juridico DePlacido e Silva, ed., Rio de Janeiro: 1961 Portuguese-Portuguese.

Portuguese: Medical

Dicionario Medical Rio de Janeiro: Editora Guanabara-Koogan 1979

Portuguese: Technical

De Pina's Technical Dictionary New York: McGraw-Hill 1975
Portuguese-English, English-Portuguese.
Dicionario de Termos Tecnicos Mendes Antas, Luis, ed., Sao Paulo:
Traco Editora 1980

RUSSIAN

General Dictionaries

Elsevier's Russian-English Dictionary. 4 vols. Macura, P., Amsterdam: Elsevier 1990 *One of the major all-around Russian-English dictionaries. Expensive.*
The Oxford Russian-English Dictionary Wheeler, M., Oxford: Clarendon Press 1984 *Excellent, but not as extensive as the Elsevier.*
English-Russian/Russian-English Dictionary Katzner, Kenneth, New York: John Wiley & Sons 1984 *Good for American English.*
New English-Russian Dictionary Galperin, I.R., Moscow: Russkiy yazyk 1988 *Reliable, one of the best in the field.*
Slovar russkogo yazyka Ozhegov, S.I., Moscow: Russkiy yazyk 1978 Russian-Russian. *A good one-volume general dictionary.*
Slovar russkogo yazyka, Rus-Rus. 4 vols., USSR Academy of Sciences Institute of Languages, Moscow: Russkiy yazyk 1981 *A first choice for many translators.*
Slovar trudnostey russkogo yazyka Rozental, D.E. Moscow: Russkiy yazyk 1976 *Very helpful for translation into Russian.*
Dictionary of Russian Abbreviations Scheitz, E., New York: Elsevier 1985 *A must. Abbreviations and acronyms are a plague of the Russian language, and a translator's nightmare.*
Russian-English Dictionary of Interjections and Response Phrases Kveselevich, D. I.; Sasina, V. P., Moscow: Russkiy yazyk 1990
Krylatyye slova: Literaturnyye tsitaty: Obraznyye vyrazheniya Ashukin, N.S., Moscow: Khudozhestvennaya literatura 1986
Frazeologicheskiy slovar russkogo yazyka Molotov, A.I., ed. Moscow: Sovetskaya entsiklopediya 1967
Slovar russkikh lichnykh imyen Petrovskiy, N.A. Moscow: Russkiy yazyk 1984
Sovetskiy entsiklopedicheskiy slovar Prokhorov, A.M., Moscow: Sovetskaya entsiklopediya 1984
Russko-angliyskiy slovar Smirnitskiy, Moscow: Russkiy yazyk 1987
Russian-English Dictionary A.M. Taube, Moscow: Russkiy yazyk
Solzhenitsyn's Peculiar Vocabulary: Russian-English Glossary Carpovich, Vera V., New York: Technical Dictionaries Co. 1976

Russian: Agriculture

Russko-angliyskiy selskokhozyaystvenniy slovar Ussovskiy 1977

Russian: Aviation/Aerospace

English-Russian Dictionary of Civil Aviation Marassanov, V.P. Moscow: Russky Yazyk Publishers 1989

Russian: Economic

Russian-English Foreign Trade and Foreign Economic Dictionary Zhdanova, I.F., Moscow: Russkiy yazyk 1991
Russian-English Foreign Trade and Foreign Economic Dictionary Zhdanova, I. F., Moscow: Russkiy yazyk 1991
Ekonomicheskiy morskoy slovar-spravochnik Kotlubay, M., Odessa: Izd. Mayak 1976
Ekonomiko-matematicheskiy slovar N. P. Fedorenko, ed., Moscow: Nauka 1987
Kratkiy ekonomicheskiy slovar Belik, Yu. A., ed., Moscow: Politizdat 1987

Russian: Education

Lingvo-stranovedcheskiy slovar: narodnoye obrazovaniye v SSSR Denisova, M.A., Moscow: Russkiy yazyk 1978

Russian: Electronics

Anglo-russkiy slovar po radioelektronike Lisovskiy, F.V., Moscow: Russkiy yazyk 1987 *A valuable and comprehensive reference in the field. Contains a Russian index.*
Anglo-russkiy slovar po mikroelektronike Prokhorov, K.Ya., Moscow: Russkiy yazyk 1985
Russian-English Dictionary of Electrotechnology and Allied Sciences Macura, P., Melbourne, FL: Robert E. Krieger Publishing Company 1986

Russian: Geology

Geologicheskiy slovar 2 vols., Moscow: 1978 Russian-Russian.
Russko-angliyskiy geologicheskiy slovar Sofiano, T. A. 1984

Russian: Law

Encyclopedia of Soviet Law Amsterdam: Martinus-Jijhoff Publishing Co. 1985

Russian: Mathematics

Russian-English Mathematical Dictionary Milne, Madison: University of Wisconsin Press 1962
Russian-English Dictionary of the Mathematical Sciences Lohwater, A.J., Providence, Rhode Island: The American Mathematical Society 1961

Russian: Medicine

Anglo-russkiy slovar po immunologii i immunogenetike Petrov, Moscow: Russkiy yazyk 1990
Anglo-russkiy slovar po biotekhnologii Drygin Moscow: Russkiy yazyk 1990
Russian-English Medical Dictionary Yeliseyenkov,Yu.B. Moscow: Russkiy yazyk 1975
Anglo-russkiy meditsinskiy slovar Akzhigitov, G.N. Moscow: Russkiy yazyk 1988 *The above four dictionaries are an absolute must for translating medical texts.*
Russian-English Biological-Medical Dictionary Carpovich, New York: Technical Dictionaries 1960
Entsiklopedicheskiy slovar meditsinskikh terminov Petrovskiy, Moscow: Sovetskaya entsiklopediya 1983   Russian-Russian

Russian: Oil

Russko-angliyskiy neftepromyslovyy slovar Stoliarov, D.E. Moscow: Russkiy yazyk 1982
Petrologicheskiy anglo-russkiy tolkovyy slovar Marakushev, A. A., ed. Moscow: Mir 1986

Russian: Physics

Russian-English Physics Dictionary Emin, Wiley 1963

Russian: Technical

Anglo-russkiy slovar po nadezhnosti i kontrolyu kachestva Kovalenko, E.G. Moscow: Russkiy yazyk 1975 *A comprehensive work for anyone engaged in this field.*

Russian-English Chemical and Polytechnical Dictionary Callaham, L., New York: Wiley, 1975 *Long used by American translators of Russian, but mainly for lack of a better technical dictionary.*

Russian-English Scientific and Technical Dictionary, 1st ed. Alford & Alford, Oxford: Pergamon 1970

Kratkiy illyustrirovannyy russko-angliyskiy slovar po mashinostroyeniyu Shvarts, V.V. Moscow: Russkiy yazyk 1983

Russko-angliyskiy tekhnicheskiy slovar Chemukhin, Moscow: Voyenizdat 1971

Politekhnicheskiy slovar Ishlinskiy Moscow: Sovetskaya entsiklopediya 1980

Russko-angliyskiy politekhnicheskiy slovar Kuznetsov, B. V. Moscow: Russkiy yazyk 1986

Anglo-russkiy slovar po sistemnomu analizu Vyshinskaya Ye. V., ed., 1982

SPANISH

General Dictionaries

Diccionario internacional Simon and Schuster T. de Gamez, New York: Simon & Schuster, 1994   English-Spanish/Spanish-English *Excellent general-purpose source for the varieties of Spanish used throughout Latin America.*
Collins Spanish-English English-Spanish Dictionary, Unabridged - Third Edition, C. Smith, New York: HarperCollins, 1993   *Widely considered one of the best of its kind.*
Larousse gran diccionario R. Garcia-Pelayo, Mexico: Ediciones Larousse, 1983   *Very comprehensive, more European-oriented than the above two.*
Diccionario de la lengua española Spanish-Spanish - 21st edition, Madrid: Real Academia de la Lengua Española, 1992
This is the official dictionary of the Spanish language. Expensive.
Gran diccionario español-inglés Garcia Pelayo y Gross, Ediciones Larousse 1983
Diccionario de uso del español Moliner, M., Madrid: Editorial Gredos 1980   Spanish-Spanish.
Diccionario enciclopédico ilustrado de la lengua española Sopena, Ramon, ed., Barcelona: 1957   Spanish-Spanish.
Diccionario de los idiomas inglés y español Velázquez, M., Englewood Cliffs, NJ: Prentice-Hall 1972   Spanish-English, English-Spanish   *Old, but still useful.*
Qué es qué (What's What), Enciclopedia visual bilingüe Maplewood, NJ: Hammond, 1988   *A pictorial dictionary.*
Visual Dictionary Corbeil, J.C., New York: Facts on File 1992
Sinónimos Castellanos Garcia, R., Sopena, R., ed., Buenos Aires 1967   Spanish-Spanish.
The Collins Spanish Dictionary Barcelona: Ediciones Grijalbo 1988 *Good for Spanish for Spain.*
Diccionario de dudas y dificultades de la lengua española Seco, M., Madrid: Espasa-Calpe 1987
Diccionario de uso del español Moliner, M., Madrid: Editorial Gredos 1987
2001 Spanish and English Idioms E. Savaiano, L. Winget,

Woodbury, NY, Barron, 1976   *Not exhaustive, but quite useful.*

General Regional Spanish Dictionaries:

Diccionario de Mejicanismos Santamaria, F., Mexico City: Editorial Porrua 1974   *Very useful for any Mexico-related translation.*
Lexicón de colombianismos vol. 1 and 2, Banco de la República, Bogota: Biblioteca Luis-Angel Arango 1983
Diccionario de venezolanismos vol. 1, A-1, Academia Venezolana de la Lengua, Universidad Central de Venezuela, Facultad de Humanidades y Educación, Caracas: Instituto de Filología Andrés Bello 1983
In progress: Cuban and Peruvian Spanish dictionaries by Anthony T. Rivas (Ref. ATA).

Spanish: Chemical

Hawley - Diccionario de química y de productos químicos Sax, I., Barcelona: Ediciones Omega 19993   *Best of its kind.*

Spanish: Computers

Diccionario de microinformática, Ing-Esp R. Tapias, Barcelona, Editorial Noray, 1985   *Old but useful.*
Diccionario de informática ing-esp Olivetti, Barcelona, Editorial Paraninfo, 1993
Dictionary of Computer Terms Chiri, A., New York: Hippocrene, 1993
Diccionario comentado de terminología informática Aguado, G., Madrid: Editorial Paraninfo 1994
Diccionario de informática ing-esp, esp-ing Madrid: Ediciones Diaz de Santos 1993

Spanish: Economic

Dictionary of Modern Business Robb, L., Washington D.C.: Anderson Kramer Associates 1960   English-Spanish, Spanish-English.
Nuevo diccionario bilingüe de economía y empresa Iruste, J., Madrid: Ediciones Piramide 1993   English-Spanish, Spanish-Eng.
Dictionary of Business Collin, P.H., Middlesex, England: 1993 English-Spanish, Spanish-English.

Harrap's Glossary of Spanish Commercial and Industrial Terms Rodrigues, L., London: Harrap 1990   English-Spanish, Sp-Eng.
Diccionario comercial ing-esp esp-ing Giraud, A., Barcelona: Editorial Juventud 1990.
English-Spanish Banking Dictionary Esteban, R.G., Madrid: Editorial Paraninfo 1993

Spanish: Engineering

Dictionary of Environmental Engineering J. Villate, Miami, Ediciones Universal, 1979
Diccionario técnico ing-esp Malgorn, G., Madrid: Paraninfo 1991
Diccionario de ingeniería Villate, J.T., Miami: Ediciones universal 1979
Engineers' Dictionary Robb, L., New York: John Wiley 1976 English-Spanish, Spanish-English.

Spanish: Legal

Diccionario de términos legales Robb, Louis A., Mexico: Editorial Limusa 1980
Diccionario de Derecho Rafael de Pina and Rafael de Pina Vara, Mexico City: Editorial Porrua 1985
Dictionary of Law, Economics and Politics Ramon Lacasa Navarro Madrid: Editoriales de Derecho Reunidas 1989

Spanish: Maritime

Diccionario marítimo y de construcción naval Perez, J. A., Barcelona: Ediciones Garriga 1976

Spanish: Medical

Diccionario de términos médicos Torres, R., Madrid: Alhambra 1989 Spanish-English, English-Spanish. *Best of its kind.*

Spanish: Military

Diccionario técnico militar A. Gomez, Madrid: Ediciones Agullo, 1980
Diccionario moderno de tecnología militar R. Wells, Fairfax, VA:

Lexicon Press, 1977

Spanish: Technical

Nuevo diccionario politécnico de las lenguas española e inglesa 2 vols., Atienza, F. B., Madrid: Diaz de Santos 1988 *For the technical translator, this dictionary is one of the best all-around Spanish-English, English-Spanish sources. Expensive.*

Glosario español-inglés de términos técnicos Spanish-English/English-Spanish, 5 vols. Thomann, Arthur E., Armco Steel Corporation 1975

Diccionario de términos científicos y técnicos 5 vols., Barcelona: McGraw-Hill Boixarev 1981 *A translation of the excellent McGraw-Hill **Dictionary of Science and Technology** (see General References).*

Spanish-English/Eng-Span Encyclopedic Dictionary of Technical Terms, 3 vols., Javier L. Collazo, McGraw-Hill 1980

Diccionario técnico Rafael Garcia Diaz, Mexico: LIMUSA, S.A. 1980

Diccionario para electrónica, telecomunicaciones e informática Buenos Aires: EMEDE, S.A. 1986

APPENDIX 2.

DICTIONARY SOURCES

Dictionaries are becoming more and more available in general bookstores, and in bookstore chains such as Borders, Barnes & Noble, Crown Books, B. Dalton, Walden, to mention a few. The following is a partial list of book sources that specialize in dictionaries, particularly hard-to-find technical dictionaries. Some, like i.b.d. Ltd. in Kinderhook, NY, will order a great many technical dictionaries for you from sources in both the U.S. and abroad. Some of the British, European and other overseas bookstores listed here are excellent, and well worth contacting.

U.S. Sources of dictionaries:

Nippon Book Company, 364 East First St., Los Angeles, CA 90012
The French & Spanish Corp., 652 S. Olive St., Los Angeles, CA 90014
German & International Book Store, 1767 N Vermont Ave., Los Angeles, CA 90027
China Books & Periodicals, Inc., 2929 24th St., San Francisco, CA 94110
Szwede Slavic Books, PO Box 1214, Palo Alto, CA 94302

Western Continental Book, Inc., 625 E. 70th Ave. #5, Denver, Colorado 80229

International Learning Center, 1715 Connecticut Ave. N.W., Washington D.C. 20009
Modern Language Book Store, Inc., 3160 "O" St., Washington D.C. 20007
Viktor Kamkin, Inc. (Russian books), 12224 Parklawn Dr., Rockville, MD 20852
Travel Books & Language Center, 4931 Cordell Ave., Bethesda, MD 20814

Ediciones Universal, PO Box 353, Miami, FL 33145

Europa Books, 915 Foster St., Evanston, IL 60201

Polonia Bookstore and Publishers Co., 2886 Milwaukee Ave., Chicago, IL 60618

Rizzoli International Bookstore, 835 N. Michigan Ave., Chicago, IL 60611

Technical Dictionaries Co., Box 2130, Mt Vernon, Maine 04352

Cheng & Tsui Co. PO Box 328, Cambridge, MA 02139

Oriental Research Partners, Publishers and Library Wholesalers, Box 158,489 Walnut St., Newtonville, MA 02160

Schoenhors Foreign Books, 1280 Massachusetts Ave., Cambridge, MA 02138

i.b.d. Ltd., International Book Distributors, 24 Hudson St., Kinderhook, NY 12106

FAM Book Service, 69 Fifth Ave., New York, NY 10003

Rizzoli International Book Store, 712 5th Ave., New York, NY 10019

Marlin Publications International, Inc., 485 Fifth Ave., New York, NY 10017

Hippocrene Books, 171 Madison Ave., New York, NY 10016

The French & Spanish Book Corporation, 115 Fifth Ave., New York, NY 10003

Eliseo Torres Spanish & Portuguese Book Center, 17 East 22d St., New York, NY 10010

Albert J. Phiebig, Inc., Box 352, White Plains, NY 10602

E.J. Brill, PO Box 1305, Long Island City, N.Y. 11101

Japan Publications Trading Co., 200 Clearbrook Rd., Elmsford, NY 10423

Slavica Publishers, PO Box 14388, Columbus, Ohio 43214

Multilingual Matters, c/o Taylor & Francis, 1900 Frost Rd., Suite 101, Bristol, PA 19007

Imported Books, PO Box 4414, Dallas, Texas 75208

Foreign Dictionary Sources:

France

La Maison du Dictionnaire, 98 Bd du Montparnasse, F 75 014 Paris, France
Editions du CNRS, 15 quai Anatole France, 75700 Paris, France
Editions Klincksieck, 11 rue de Lille, 75007 Paris, France

Germany

Alexander Horn, Internationale Buchhandlung, Friedrichstrasse 39, Postfach 3340, 6200 Wiesbaden, Germany
Kubon & Sagner, Postfach 340108, **D 8000**, **Munchen** 34, Germany
Otto Harrassowitz, Internationale Buchhandlung, Asien-Abteilung Postfach 2929, Taunusstrasse 5, Germany

Hong Kong

Joint Publishing Company, Readers Service Centre, 9 Victoria St., Central District, Hong Kong

Sweden

Tekniska Litteratursallskapet, Box 5073, 102 42 Stockholm, Sweden

United Kingdom

B.H. Blackwell, Ltd, 48-51 Broad St., Oxford, OX 1 3BQ United Kingdom
Bailey Bros. and Swinfen, Ltd., Warner House, Bowles Well Gardens, Folkestone, Kent CT19 6PH, United Kingdom
Orbis Books (London) Ltd, 66 Kenway Rd., London SW5 ORD, England
Grant & Cutler, 55-57 Great Marlborough St., London W1V 2AY, England
Interpress Ltd., 179 Blythe Rd., London W 14 OHL, England

APPENDIX 3.

SOURCES OF TRANSLATION WORK

For general information about obtaining translation work, see Chapter 10.

There are three major sources of translation work in the United States: the government sector, the public sector, and the private sector.

The government sector ranges from the city, county and state government, to the federal government. All of them need translation work on a fairly regular basis, and all of them are worth contacting. It is not always easy to find the right person or office to contact, but perseverance does pay off. One good place to start your search is the procurement, or contracting office of any given government entity. They usually know who in the system needs what, and they can often tell you whether they've heard lately of someone in the system needing translation. Again, you need to have a great deal of patience with these folks, who are not known for their alacrity.

The U.S. Government, or the "Government" with a capital G, is a huge source of translation. It is hard to put a dollar figure on it, but it certainly goes into the many millions of dollars per year. Government translation requests come in three main forms:

a. Translation contracts. Various government agencies issue a request for a bid on a one to five year translation contract. Those usually require several languages, and most freelancers cannot handle them on their own. To find out about those contracts, read the government publication *Commerce Business Daily* (found in many public libraries). You may want to monitor the contract office handling the particular contract, and have them tell you (under the Freedom of Information Act) which company is awarded the contract. You then contact that company and offer your services in your particular areas of expertise.

b. Translation requirements in a non-translation contract. The Government may need a company to monitor drug dealers who speak Spanish. It contracts with a company specialized in electronic monitoring. That company will then subcontract the translation portion of its prime contract to a translation company. Here again you can follow this process, and offer your services.

c. One-time translation order. The Department of Energy may need to translate a Russian book on power plants. It will look for someone who has a good knowledge of Russian and English, and experience in this kind of technical translation. They usually turn to a translation company, but they may also contract with an individual. This type of assignment is very hard to find, since the agency will rarely advertise what they call a "small purchase" (which to a freelancer can be quite big), and would contact an established translation company.

The public sector includes many organizations, academic institutions, foundations, and so on. All of them, at one time or another, need translation work. The question is how to find out who needs what and when. I wish I had the answer, but I don't.

The same holds true for the private sector, which consists of commercial and industrial entities, law firms, and individuals.

All of which leaves you with the translation companies, who in effect act as a broker between you and the work sources. They develop many contacts, they bid on contracts, they advertise in the media and in the Yellow Pages, and they provide millions of dollars worth of translation work for freelancers every year.

The following is a list, arranged alphabetically by state, of translation companies. A word of caution: Not all of them are financially sound, and they do not always pay on time, or treat freelancers with the professional dignity they usually deserve. Inclusion in the ensuing list does not mean in any way that we endorse any of the companies listed. We leave it to you to check out any company you may be interested in, and establish your own relationship with them.

ALABAMA

Foreign Language Services, Inc., 3609 Memorial Pkwy SW Suite A-5, Huntsville, AL 35801
Worldwide Translation Trade Co., PO Box 16371, Mobile, AL 36616

ARIZONA

Word Communications International, 4513 N. 12 St. Phoenix, AZ 85014

CALIFORNIA

AA International Translations & Linguistics, 2312 W. Artesia Blvd. Suite 104, Redondo Beach, CA 90278

Allied Interpreting & Translating Service, PO Box 480347, Los Angeles, CA 90048

Bilingual Services, 2060 Cedar Ave., Long Beach, CA 90806

Diversified Language Institute, 1670 Wilshire Blvd, Los Angeles, CA 90017

East West Institute, 110 N. Berendo St. Los Angeles, CA 90004

English Language Center, 1256 Westwood Blvd., Los Angeles, CA 90024

Foreign Language Graphics, 4303 N. Figueroa St., Los Angeles, CA 90065

International Translation Bureau, 125 W. 4th St. Suite 240 Los Angeles, CA 90013

International Documentation, 10474 Santa Monica Blvd. #404 Los Angeles, CA 90025

International School of Languages, PO Box 6188, Beverly Hills, CA 90212

Intex Translations, 9021 Melrose Ave. Suite 205 Los Angeles, CA 90069

Leo Rosenblum & Associates, 5150 Wilshire Blvd, #506, Los Angeles, CA 90036

Lingualink, 5777 W. Century Blvd. Suite 1107 Los Angeles, CA 90045

Linguistica International, 3486 Military Ave., Los Angeles, CA 90034

Pan Pacific Link, 4525 Wilshire Blvd., Los Angeles, CA 90010

Paragon, 6500 Wilshire Blvd., #300, Los Angeles, CA 90048

Rancho Park Publishing, 11766 Wilshire Blvd. Suite 310, Los Angeles, CA 90025

Services Unlimited, 205 S. Beverly Dr. Suite 210 Beverly Hills, CA 90212

TLS, PO Box 34950, Los Angeles, CA 90034

WORDEXPRESS, 513 Wilshire Blvd, suite 290 Santa Monica, CA 90401

Atlas Services, 336 N. Central Ave. Suite 9, Glendale, CA 91203

Berlitz, 6150 Canoga Ave., Woodland Hills, CA 91367
Beyond Words Translation, PO Box 15992, North Hollywood, CA 91615
ComNet International, 30941 W. Agoura Rd., Suite 124, Westlake Village, CA 91361
Continental Communications Agency, 7120 Hayvenhurst Suite 205, Van Nuys, CA 91406
CSA Interpreting, 1695 N. Francis Ave. Upland, CA 91784
G T Translation Services, Inc., 10970 Arrow Route, #104, Rancho Cucamonga, CA 91730
Inlingua Training and Translation Services, 101 N. Brand Blvd., Suite 930, Glendale, CA 91203
Interpreting Services International, PO Box 618, Van Nuys, CA 91408
Omega Business Services, Inc. 223 South Brand Blvd., Suite 213 Glendale, CA 91204
Omni Interpreting and Translating Network, PO Box 3549, Westlake Village, CA 91359
Universal Translation Agency, PO Box 19035, Encino, CA 91416

Affinity Language Services, PO Box 2408, Del Mar, CA 92014
American Translation Services, 4401 Manchester, Suite 105, Encinitas, CA 92024
Berlitz, 7801 Mission Center Court, San Diego, CA 92108
Business Spoken Here, 2921 Nutmeg Street, San Diego, CA 92104
Certified Interpreters & Translators, 5946 Albemarle St., PO Box 390006, San Diego, CA 92149
GARJAK International, Inc., 5330 Caffoll Canyon Road, Ste 101, San Diego, CA 92121
Inlingua, 8950 Villa La Jolla Dr. Suite 21 10 La Jolla, CA 92037
International Word Factory, 4958 Marlborough Dr., San Diego, CA 92116
International Word Factory, 4958 Marlborough Dr., San Diego, CA 92116
Interpreters Unlimited, 16835 West Bernado Dr., Suite 205 San Diego, CA 92127
Interpreters Unlimited, 16835 West Bernado Dr. Suite 205 San Diego, CA 92127

Linguistic Translation Service, 2515 Camino Del Rio S., Suite 113, San Diego, CA 92108

Multilingual Translations, 7676 Hazard Center Dr., Ste 1515 San Diego, CA 92108

Sally Low and Associates, 600 W. Santa Ana Blvd., Suite #208, Santa Ana, CA 92701

The Language Connection, PO Box 1962, Laguna Beach, CA 92652

Translingua, P. 0. Box 1662, Rancho Santa Fe, CA 92067

Trans Pacific Communications, 192 Technology Dr, Suite G, Irvine, CA 92718

AT&T Language Line Services, 1 Lower Ragsdale Dr., Bldg. 2 Suite 400, Monterey, CA 93940

Language Services International, 26555 Carmel Rancho Blvd., Suite 5-B, Carmel, CA 93923

Lourdes Gonzalez de Campbell Interpreting, 674 County Square Dr., Ste. 305, Ventura, CA 93003

Omega International, 467 Alvarado St., Ste. 21, Monterey, CA 93940

Scitran, 1482 East Valley Road, PO Box 5456, Santa Barbara, CA 93108

Transpefect, 2536 Barstow Ave., Clovis, CA 93611

Ad-Ex Worldwide, 525 Middlefield Rd., Suite 150, Menlo Park, CA 94025

Benemann Translation Center, 760 Market St., Suite 1000, San Francisco, CA 94102

Berkeley Scientific Translation Service, Inc., PO Box 318, Berkeley, CA 94701

BioMedical Translations, 3477 Kenneth Dr., Palo Alto, CA 94303

California Translation International, 1904 Olympic Blvd., #12 Walnut Creek, CA 94596

Costa Foreign Language Service, Inc., 191 Fairmont Avenue, San Carlos, CA 94070

Dial-an-Interpreter, Opera Plaza #409, 601 Van Ness, San Francisco, CA 94102

Direct Language Communications, 301 Mission St., Suite 350, San Francisco, CA 94105

Geonexus Communications, 522 Ramona St., Palo Alto, CA 94301

Idem Translation Center, 614 Greer Road, Palo Alto, CA 94303

In Other Words, PO Box 606, Berkeley, CA 94701

International Contact, Inc., World Savings Tower, 1970 Broadway, Suite 315, Oakland, CA 94612

JLS Language Associates, 135 Willow Rd., Menlo Park, CA 94025

KISFFIV Channel, 26 100 Valley Drive, Brisbane, CA 94005

KTSF/TV Channel, 26 100 Valley Drive Brisbane, CA 94005

Lan Do and Associates Language Services, 25 Stillman St., Suite 106, San Fancisco, CA 94107

Language Bank, 875 O'Farrell St., Suite 105, San Francisco, CA 94109

Leo Kanner Assocs., 1800 Broadway, Suite 3, PO Box 5187, Redwood City, CA 94063

Polyglot International, 340 Brannan St., 5th Floor, San Francisco, CA 94107

Tradux, 235 Montgomery, Suite 1126, San Francisco, CA 94104

Translations Express!! Auerbach International, Inc., 2031 Union St., Suite 2, San Francisco, CA 94123

Tristan Translations, 1130 Taylor St., San Francisco, CA 94108

Alpha Language Group, Attn: Claude St. Mars, 1560 Oak St., Oroville, CA 95965

Century School of Languages Translating Service, 1066 Saratoga Ave., Suite 220, San Jose, CA 95129

HighTech Passport, 1590 Oakland Rd., Suite B-208, San Jose, CA 95131

International Accessability Corp., 500 Chestnut Street, Suite 200, Santa Cruz, CA 95060

International Translation Service, PO Box 188331, Sacramento, CA 95818

Language Dynamics, 931 Howe Ave., #107, Sacramento, CA 95825

Total Translating Service, PO Box 188487, Sacramento, CA 95818

Transcend, 1138 Villaverde St., Davis, CA 95616

Wordmill, PO Box 1817, Healdsburg, CA 95448

COLORADO

A B C Translating Service, 5595 Federal Blvd., Denver, CO 80221

Accura International Language Services, 12862 Cherry Way
Thomton, CO 80241
Cosmopolitan Business Communication, 8025 Marshall Circle,
Arvada, CO 80003
Delta Translation International, 1900 Wazee St., #1543
Denver, CO 80202
Escalante International Corp., 1665 Grant St., Denver, CO 80203
Linguex Translation Services, 1325 S. Colorado Blvd., Denver, CO
80222
SEI Foreign Language Services, 5757 Central Ave., Suite G, Boulder,
CO 80301

CONNECTICUT

Accent, Inc., 345 N. Main St., West Hartford, CT 06117
Global Language Management, 239 Mill St., Greenwich, CT 06830
Inlingua, 2701 Summer St., Stamford, CT 06905
Inlingua, 45 S. Main St., #100, West Hartford, CT 06107
L'express International, Inc., PO Box 4234, Greenwich, CT 06830
The Language Center Inc., 2 Benedict Place, Greenwich, CT 06830

DISTRICT OF COLUMBIA

Allied languages Cooperative, 2714 31st St. SE, $662, Washington,
DC 20020
Berlitz, 1730 Rhode Island Ave. NW, Washington, DC 20036
Center for Applied Linguistics, 1118 22nd St. NW, Washington, DC
20037
CyberTrans International, Inc. 1100 Connecticut Ave. NW Ste. 520
Washington, DC 20036
Galaxy Systems, 2004 17th St. NW, Washington, DC 20009
German Translation & Interpreting, 4925 Upton St. NW, Washington,
DC 20016
Inlingua, 1030 15th St. NW, Washington, DC 20005
International Translation Center, 1660 L St. NW, Rm. 613,
Washington, DC 20036
Kompass Resources International, 1322 18th St. NW, Washington, DC
20036
Language Learning Enterprises, 1100 17th St. NW, #900, Washington,
DC 20036

Language Doctors, 410 11th St. NE, Washington, DC 20002
LanguagExchange, 1821 18th St. NW, Washington, DC 20009
Linguex, 1612 K St. NW, Suite 700, Washington, DC 20006
Linx Interpretation Services, 1609 Connecticut Ave. NW, Suite 310, Washington, DC 20009
Transemantics, Inc., 4301 Connecticut Ave., NW Suite 146, Washington, DC 20008
Victoria Enterprises, 1735 I St. NW, Washington, DC 20006

FLORIDA

A to Z Translation and Professional Services, 13521 SW 113th Pl, Miami, FL 33176
A to Z Word-O-Matics, 9100 S. Dadeland Blvd, Miami, FL 33156
A L Madrid & Associates, 340 Minorca Ave., Suite 4, Coral Gables, FL 33134
A Gift of Tongues, 2301 SW 20th St., Miami, FL 33145
A B Professional Services Translating Co., 9485 SW 72nd St., Miami, FL 33173
A B SI Translation Services, 8350 NW 52nd Ter. #209, Miami, FL 33166
A-Mundial Milti-Service Agency, 742 NW 12th Ave., Miami, FL 33136
ABC Services, Inc., 561 NE 79th St., Miami, FL 33138
Acclimatizing Services International, 1975 NE 6th St., Deerfield Beach, FL 33441
Accredited Translators & Certified Interpreters, Inc., 66 SW 32 Ave., Miami, FL 33135
Action Translation Services, 6595 NW 36th St., Miami, FL 33166
Advanced Translation, Inc., 233 80th St., Miami Beach, FL 33141
Albors and Associates, Inc., PO Box 5516, Winter Park, FL 32793
Alpha Language Services, 4728 SW 67th Ave., Miami, FL 33155
American Video Language Institute, 3909 NE 163rd St., N. Miami Beach, FL 33160
Berlitz, 396 Alhambra Circle, Coral Gables, Fl 33134
Expert Translators, 11430 N. Kendall Dr., Suite 212, Miami, FL 33176
Global Institute of Languages and Culture, Inc., 300 S. Pine Island

Rd., Plantation, FL 33324
Hold Translations, 1010 Dupont Plaza Center, Miami, FL 33131
Inlingua, 1000 Brickell Ave., Suite 105 Miami, FL 33131
Marsh, Inc., 660 NE 78th St. Suite 305, Miami, FL 33138
Master Translating Services, Inc., 10651 N. Kendall Dr., Suite 220, Miami, FL 33176
Mitchell Translations, Inc., 4155 East View Pl., Gulf Breeze, FL 32561
Professional Translating Services, Inc., 44 W. Flagler St., Suite 540, Miami, FL 33130
Seven Languages Translating, Inc., 155 S. Miami Ave., Miami, FL 33130
Sykes Enterprises, Inc., 100 N. Tampa St., Suite 3900, Tampa, FL 33602
The Language Solution, Inc., 490 E. Palmetto Park Rd., Boca Raton, FL 33432
TIICO-Translating Interpreting International Co., PO Box 61613, Fort Myers, FL 33906

GEORGIA

Access Translations, Peachtree Road NE, Suite D331, Atlanta, GA 30309
Bilingual Atlanta, 627 Cherokee St., Suite 15, Marietta, GA 30060
GlobalDoc Inc., 1800 Peachtree St., Suite 370, Atlanta, GA 30309
Inlingua Translation, 3384 Peachtree Rd. NE, Suite 560, Atlanta, GA 30326
Language Services, 2256 Northlake Pkwy., Suite 309, Tucker, GA 30084
Tartir International Services, 1225 Johnson Ferry Rd., Suite 700, Marietta, GA 30068
The Kaspi Group International, 750 Hammond Dr., Bldg. 6, Atlanta, GA 30328

ILLINOIS

Advance Language Interlingua, 333 North Michigan, Suite 3200, Chicago, IL 60601
Nelles Translations, 18 S. Michigan, Room 1000, Chicago, IL 60603

Academy of Legal & Technical Translations, 9354 Avers Ave., Evanston, IL 60203

ACCESS Medical Communications, 3880 RFD Salem Lake Drive, Suite A, Long Grove, IL 60047

Action Translation Bureau, 7825 W. 101 St., Palos Hills, IL 60465

Active Communications Bureau, 401 N. Franklin, Chicago, IL 60610

Berlitz, 2 N LaSalle St., Chicago, IL 60602

Burg Translation Bureau, Inc., One First National Plaza, Suite 2650 Chicago, IL 60603

Cosmopolitan, 53 W. Jackson, Suite 1260, Chicago, IL 60604

Domenech & Assoc, PO Box 641532, Chicago, IL 60664

Inlingua, 20 N. Michigan Ave., Suite 560, Chicago, IL 60602

International Business Communication, 625 N. Michigan, Suite 500, Chicago, IL 60611

Lingua Communications Translation Services, 9321 Lavergne, Suite 101, Skokie, IL 60077

Nael International Translators, 6347 N. Rockwell, Chicago, IL 60659

Quest Technology, Inc., 1030 West Higgins, Suite 355 Park Ridge, IL 60068

Technical Scientific Translation, 5323 Davis St., Skokie, IL 60077

Techno-Graphics and Translation, 1451 E. 168th St., South Holland, IL 60473

TLI International Corp., 680 N. Lake Shore Dr., Suite 1220, Chicago, IL 60611

INDIANA

International Bureau of Translations, Inc., 3254 N. Washington Blvd., Indianapolis, IN 46205

Prolingua, 50 E. 91st St. #209, Indianapolis, IN 46240

IOWA

OmniLingua, Inc., 2857 Mount Vernon Road, S.E., Cedar Rapids, IA 52403

LOUISIANA

Modern Languages Institute, 1208 St. Charles Ave., New Orleans, LA 70130

Professional Translators and Interpreters, Inc., 1042 World Trade Center, New Orleans, LA 70130

MARYLAND

Academy of Languages, 2116 N. Charles St., Baltimore, MD 21218
Contact International Inc., PO Box 2313, Baltimore, MD 21203
Geiger Associates, 5011 Westport Ct., Chevy Chase, MD 20815
Inlingua, 10451 Mill Run Cirle, Owings Mill, MD 21117
International Language Center, 2266 Glenmore Terrace, Rockville, MD 20850
Linguamatics, Inc., 414 Hungerford Dr. Suite 206, Rockville, MD 20850
M2 Ltd., PO Box 2342, Gaithersburg, MD 20886
Pacifica Corp., 3300 N. Ridger Rd., Ellicott City, MD 21043
Schreiber Translations, Inc. PO Box 2142, Rockville, MD 20847
The Language Institute, 1055 Taylor Ave., Suite 301, Towson, MD 21286
The Language Institute, Inc., 1055 Taylor Ave., #301, Towson, MD 21204
Translingua, Inc., 5457 Twin Knolls Rd. Columbia, MD 21045

MASSACHUSETTS

Adaptive Language Resources, Inc., 955 Massachusetts Ave., Suite 334, Cambridge, MA 02139
Boston School of Modern Languages, 240 Commonwealth Ave., Boston, MA 02116
Cambridge Translation Resources, 186 South Street Boston, MA 02111
Crimson Language Services, Inc., 258 Harvard St., Suite 305 Brookline, MA 02146
Dovali Translations Inc., 173 Washington St., Hudson, MA 01749
Global Solutions, 36 Washington St., Wellesley Hills, MA 02181
Hablespana, 89 Broad St. Suite 1103A, Boston, MA 02110
Harvard Translations, 137 Newbury St., Boston, MA 02116
Inlingua Translations, 31 St. James Ave., Suite 907, Boston, MA 02116
International Documentation Services, 1 Kendall Sq., Suite 2200 Cambridge, MA 02139
International Communications, Inc., 1 Apple Hill, Natick, MA 01760

Intransco, PO Box 5419, Magnolia, MA 01930
Language Consultants, 167 Worcester Rd., Wellesley Hills, MA 02181
Linguistic Systems, Inc., 130 Bishop Allen Dr, Cambridge, MA 02139
Poly-Lingua, World Trade Ctr., Suite 125, Boston, MA 02210
Rapport International, 3 Stonegate Lane, Middleboro, MA 02346
Speak Easy Language Solutions, One Kendall Sq., Suite 2200, Cambridge, MA 02139
The Translators, 458 Boston Street, Suite 4, PO Box 303, Topsfield, MA 01983
Trancorp International, Inc., 8 Fanneuil Hall Marketplace, 3rd fl., Boston, MA 02109
Transtek Associates, PO Box 2126, Woburn, MA 01888
WORDNET, Inc., 30 Nagog Park, Suite 200, Acton, MA 01720

MICHIGAN

AA Translation Express, 1018 Gott St., Ann Arbor, MI 48103
AAA Language Services, 3250 W. Big Beaver, Suite 120, Troy, MI 48084
Detroit Translation Bureau, 3310 W. Big Beaver Rd., Sheffield Office Park, Suite 543, Troy, MI 48084
Foreign Language Studios, 17360 W. 12 Mile Rd., Southfield, MI 48076
International Translating Bureau, 16125 W. 12 Mile Rd., Southfield, MI 48076
International Communications and Language Services, 15139
International Language Services, 352 S. Saginaw St. Suite 1018, Flint, MI 48502
International Institute of Flint, 515 Stevens St., Flint, MI 48502
Language International, 2440 Burton St. SE, Grand Rapids, MI 49546
Language International, 2440 Burton St. SE, Grand Rapids, MI 49546
Mercury Dr., Grand Haven, MI 49417
Post Translations, 3290 S. Adams, Suite 303, Auburn Hills, MI 48326
Professional Advancement Enterprises, 2182 Saginaw SE, Grand Rapids, MI 49506
Speak Easy Languages, 757 S. Main St., Plymouth, MI 48170
Synapse Intercultural Conimunications, 35526 Grand River Ave., Suite 347, Farmington Hills, MI 48335

Translations Unlimited, 1455 Forest Hill SE, Grand Rapids, MI 49506

MINNESOTA

A A A Worldwide Translation Center, 4524 Excelsior Blvd., #201, Minneapolis, MN 55416

Attomey's Process Service International, 7800 Glenroy Rd., Minneapolis, MN 55439

Betmar Languages, PO Box 32934, Minneapolis, MN 55432

BioLingua, Inc., 130 Amherst St., St. Paul, MN 55105

Century Design, 530 15th Ave., South Hopkins, MN 55343

Communication Arts International, 280 N. Second Ave., Suite 304, Minneapolis, MN 55401

Community Interpreter Services, 970 Raymond Ave., #101, St. Paul, MN 55114

International Business Services, PO Box 13073, Minneapolis, MN 55414

International Language Services, Inc., 133 1st Ave. North, Minneapolis, MN 55401

JKW International, 1109 Nicollet Ave. #215, Minneapolis, MN 55403

Lingua Media, 219 Main St. SE Suite 310, Minneapolis, MN 55414

LinguaNet, Inc., 1120 7th Street SE, 2nd Floor, Minneapolis, MN 55414

The Bridge World Languages Services, 3339 W. St., Germaine Suite 214, St. Cloud, MN 56301

Toward, Inc., 1924 Minnesota Ave., Duluth, MN 55802

University Language Ctr., 1313 Fifth St. SE, Suite 201, Minneapolis, MN 55414

MISSOURI

Calvin International Communications, Inc., 7710 Carondelet Ave., Suite 404, St. Louis, MO 63105

International Language Center, 1418 S. Big Bend Blvd., St. Louis, MO 63117

SH3, 5338 E. 115 St., Kansas City, MO 64137

Transimpex Translations, 8301 E. 166 St., Belton, MO 64012

NEBRASKA

The International Word, 4813 Douglas St., Omaha, NE 68132

NEW JERSEY

Al Documentation Associates, 231 Nassau St., Princeton, NJ 08542
Allen Translation Service, Box 1529, Morristown, NJ 07962
Antler Translation Services, 6 Apple Tree Ln., Suite 7, Sparta, NJ 07871
Bergen Language Institute, 555 Cedar La., Teaneck, NJ 07666
Bureau of Translation Services, 44 Tanner St., Haddonfield, NJ 08033
Conquistador Translating Service, 209 Mt. Prospect Ave., Newark, NJ 07104
Counterpoint Language Consultants, Inc., PO Box 6184, Bridgewater, NJ 08807
Cybertec, Inc., 153 W. Westfield Ave., Roselle Park, NJ 07204
East-West Concepts, Inc., 414 Plainsboro Rd., Plainsboro, NJ 08536
Inlingua Translation Service, 95 Summit Ave., Summit, NJ 07901
Inlingua Translation Services, 171 E. Ridgewood Ave., Ridgewood, NJ 07450
Inlingua, 20 Nassau St., Princeton, NJ 08542
Princeton Technical Translation Ctr., 333 Bolton Rd., East Windsor, NJ 08520
Scitech Translations, 5-21 Elizabeth St. Fair Lawn, NJ 07410
Specan International, Inc., PO Box 3111, Princeton, NJ 08543
The Language Center, 144 Tices Ln., East Brunswick, NJ 08816
Translation Company of New York, 8 South Maple Ave., Marlton, NJ 08053
Translation Plus, 7 Rt. 46 W., Lodi, NJ 07644

NEW YORK

All-Language Services, 545 Fifth Ave., New York, NY 10017
Ad Hoc Translation, Inc., 611 Broadway, Suite 803, New York, NY 10012
Accent on Language, 160 E. 56 St. 5th Fl, New York, NY 10022
Accredited Language Services, 18 John St., New York, NY 10038
Accurapid Translation Services, 806 Main St., Poughkeepsie, NY 12603
Ad-Ex Translation International, 630 5th Ave., Rm 2258, New York, NY 10111
All Major Translation, 28-02 34the Ave., Long Island City, NY 11108

American Translations & Interpreters of NY Inc., 225 Broadway #1040, New York, NY 10007

American Linguists, 200 E. 32nd St. #15D, New York, NY 10016

Asian Translators & Interpreters, 225 W. 57th St., New York, NY 10019

Berlitz, 61 Broadway, New York, NY 10006

Berlitz, 257 Park Ave. S., New York, NY 10010

Bertrand Languages, 370 Lexington Ave., New York, NY 10017

Bowne Translation Services, 345 Hudson St., New York, NY 10014

Calder Translations, Inc., 126 State St., Brooklyn, NY 11201

Cherry Valley Language Technology, 7782 Route 20, Pompey, NY 13138

Common Language, Inc., 45 W. 45th St., Suite 700, New York, NY 10036

Continental Translation Service, Inc. 6 E. 43 St., Suite 2100, New York, NY 10017

Copper Publications, 530 Franklin St., Suite 207, Schenectady, NY 12305

Corporate Language Services, 15 Maiden Ln, Suite 300, New York, NY 10038

Document Processing Center, Inc., 28 Vesey St., Suite 2112, New York, NY 10007

Di-Mar Interpreting Translating Services, 215 2nd Ave., Suite C-2, New York, NY 10003

Enterprise Translations, 400 E. 52nd Street, Suite 10K, New York, NY 10022

Eriksen Translation Inc., 32 Court St. Suite 2109 Brooklyn, NY 11201

EuroNet Language Services, 54 W. 39th St, New York, NY 10018

Foreign Translations Center, 1501 Broadway Suite 2002, New York, NY 10036

Gerard Associates Linguistic Services, 234 Fifth Ave. 2nd fl., New York, NY 10001

Globe Language Services, 319 Broadway 2nd floor, New York, NY 10007

Ibero American, 630 9th Ave., Suite 700, New York, NY 10036

Inlingua, 551 Fifth Ave., Suite 720, New York, NY 10176

InterNation Communication, Inc., 4 White St., Suite 5-B, New York, NY 10013

International Interpreter Service, 22 Summit Ave., Buffalo, NY 14214
International Institute of Buffalo, 864 Delaware Ave., Buffalo, NY 14209
Interpreters International & Translations, 123-40 83rd Ave., Suite 9D, Kew Gardens, NY 11415
Interspeak, 114 E. 32 St., Suite 1406, New York, NY 10016
Kern Corporation, 230 Park Avenue, Suite 925, New York, NY 10169
Lawyers & Merchants Translation Bureau, 11 Broadway, New York, NY 10004
LetterPerfect, 730 Violet Ave., Hyde Park, NY 12538
Linguistic Consulting Enterprises, Ltd., 64 Revolutionary Rd., Ossining, NY 10562
Linguistic Services for Professionals, Inc., 625 Main St., Suite LL-40, Roosevelt Island, NY 10044
Marion Rosley Secretarial Services, 41 Topland Rd., Hartsdale, NY 10530
Metropolitan Interpreters and Translators, 310 Madison Ave., Suite 706, New York, NY 10017
Rennert Bilingual Translations, 2 W. 45th St., New York, NY 10036
Simultaneous Wireless Interpretations, 305 Broadway Suite, 408 New York, NY 10007
Spanish Language Services, 18 John St., New York, NY 10038
Spectrum Multilanguage Communications, 225 West 39th St., New York, NY 10018
TCA, 10 West 37 St., New York, NY 10018
The Language Lab, 211 East 43rd St., #1904, New York, NY 10017
Translation Co. of America, 10 W. 37th St., New York, NY 10018
Translation Aces, Inc., 29 Broadway, Suite 1707, New York, NY 10006
Translmage Inc., 145 Hudson St., 9th Floor, New York, NY 10013
Transperect Translations International, Inc., 315 Park Ave. S, New York, NY 10010
Turkic-American Communications, 301 E. 94th St., 16-D, New York, NY 10128
WIG, 27 W. 20th St. #402, New York, NY 10011
YAR Communication Inc. 220 Fifth Ave., New York, NY 10001

NORTH CAROLINA

AT&T Business Translations, 2400 Reynolda Rd., Winston-Salem, NC 27106

Carolina Polyglot, Inc., PO Box 36334, Charlotte, NC 28236

Carolina Translation Service, Inc. 1431 Sterling Rd., Charlotte, NC 28209

Dialogos International, Inc. 5104 Oak Park Rd., Raleigh, NC 27612

DTS Language Service, Inc., 100 Europa Dr., Suite 390, Chapel Hill, NC 27515

Edward B. Rock Associates, Inc., 5200 Park Rd., Suite 200-G, PO Box 12138, Charlotte, NC 28220

Global Translation Systems Inc., 910 Airport Rd., Chapel Hill, NC 27514

OHIO

ALTCO Translations, 1426 Ridgeview Rd., Columbus, OH 43221

ASIST Translation Services, 4663 Executive Dr. Suite 11, Columbus, OH 43220

Berlitz, 580 Walnut St., Cincinnati, OH 45215

Committed To Results, Inc., 1503 Springfield Pike, Suite 110, Cincinnati, OH 45246

Conversa Language Center, 524 Walnut St., Suite 208, Cincinnati, OH 45202

Germaine Language Center, 137 N. Main St., Suite 206, Dayton, OH 45402

Inlingua Translation Service, 322 E. 4th St., Cincinnati, OH 45202

Intercontinental Service, PO Box 615, Washington Court House, OH 43160

International Institute, 2040 Scottwood Ave., Toledo, OH 43620

International Language Source, Inc., PO Box 338, Holland, OH 43528

International Lanuguage Plus, 10921 Reed Hartman Hwy, Cincinnati, OH 45242

Kindt & Co., 1965 E. 6th St., Suite 610, Cleveland, OH 44114

Lingua International, 3055 Bethel Rd., Columbus, OH 43220

Multitalk Language System, 4009 Brandy Chase Way, Cincinnati, OH 45245

Technical Translation Services, 37841 Euclid Avenue, PO Box 68,

Willoughby, OH 44094

OKLAHOMA

Calderon Language Translations, 1358 East 61st St., Tulsa, OK 74136
Inter Lingua, Inc. 4330 E. 72nd St., PO Box 700233, Tulsa, OK 74170
Language Associates, 2700 NW 49th, Oklahoma City, OK 73112
Translation Specialists, PO Box 47-1168, Tulsa, OK 74147

OREGON

ELP, L.L.C., 5100 SW Macadam Ave., Suite 450, Portland, OR 97201
International Language Bank, 1336 E. Burnside St., Portland, OR 97214
International Language Services Inc., PO Box 23922, Tigard, OR 97223
Pacific Interpreters, PO Box 601, Gresham, OR 97030
Peters Translation, 9175 SW Monterey Pl., Portland, OR 97225
SARJAM Communications Ltd., 2417 NE 51st Ave., Suite B, Portland, OR 97213
Terra Pacific Writing Corporation, PO Box 1244, Corvallis, OR 97339

PENNSYLVANIA

Berlitz Translation Services, 1608 Walnut St., Philadelphia, PA 19103
Foreign Language Institute Inc., 1510 Chestnut St., Philadelphia, PA 19102
Foreign Language Institute Inc., 1510 Chestnut St., 3rd fl., Philadelphia, PA 19102
Frank C. Farnham Company, Inc., 1930 Chestnut Street, Suite 1203, Philadelphia, PA 19103
Frank C. Famham Company, Inc., 1930 Chestnut St., Suite 1203, Philadelphia, PA 19103
GLS International Translation & Interpretation Service, 230 S. Broad St., Philadelphia, PA 19102
Inlingua Translation Service, 230 South Broad St., Philadelphia, PA 19102
Intertech Translations, 671 S. Gulph Rd., King Of Prussia, PA 19406
Languages, Inc., 725 N. 24th St., Philadelphia, PA 10130

Lexicomm International, 812 Addison St., Philadelphia, PA 19147

American Translation Company, 960 S. Braddock Ave., Pittsburgh, PA
15221
Mellon Bank Foreign Language Services, 3 Mellon Bank Center 2623,
Pittsburgh, PA 15259
Multilingual Communications Corp., 3603 Bates St., PO Box 7164,
Pittsburgh, PA 15213
The Corporate Word, Inc., 2 Gateway Center, Pittsburgh, PA 15222
American Translation Co., 960 S. Braddock Ave., Pittsburgh, PA
15221
CTI, Inc., 332 Indian Creek Dr., Mechanicsburg, PA 17055
Language Services Associates, 607 N Easton Rd. - D2 Willow Grove,
PA 19090
Professional International Enterprises, 1614 State St., Harrisburg, Pa
17103
Translex International, PO Box 1070, Benjamin Fox Pavilion
Jenkintown, PA 19046
Wehbe Translation Firm, 345 Avon St., Easton, PA 18042

RHODE ISLAND

EIEU, 645 Elmwood Ave., Providence, RI 02907
ProTrans, 97 Irving Ave., Providence, RI 02906

SOUTH CAROLINA

International Business Conununications Corp.,   PO Box 11933,
Columbia, SC 29211

TENNESSEE

AAA Translators, Inc., 3030 Elmore Park Rd., Bartlett, TN 38134
DBA International Enterprises, PO Box 240113, Memphis, TN 38124
TRANSGLOBAL Language Services, 534 Princeton Cove, Memphis,
TN 38117

TEXAS

A E Translations, 14780 Memorial Dr., Suite 202, Houston, TX 77079
Action, 2500 W. Loop South, Houston, TX 77054
American Bureau of Professional Translators, 6363 Richmond Ave.

Suite #301, Houston, TX 77057
Berlitz, 520 Post Oak Blvd., Houston, TX 77027
Foreign Language Services, 3310 Buttercup St. #6, Houston, TX 77063
Global Translation Services, 8705 Katy Fwy, Suite 204, Houston, TX 77024
Inlingua, 2500 W. Loop South, Suite 500, Houston, TX 77027
IRV, 6420 Richmond, Suite 530, Houston, TX 77057
Omni Intercommunications, Inc., 2825 Wilcrest, Suite 361 Houston, TX 77042
The Language Company, 10202 Ella Lee Ln., Houston, TX 77042
The Translation Co., 14780 Memorial Dr., Houston, TX 77079
Translations Verbatim, 725 International Blvd., Houston, TX 77024
Universe Technical Translation, 9330 Memorial Dr., Houston, TX 77024

Adams Translations, 12885 Research Blvd., Suite 206, Austin, TX 78750
ACS, 12885 Research Blvd., $206, Austin, TX 78750
Berlitz, 8400 N. Mo-Pac Expwy, Austin, TX 78759
Bilingual Services, 9407 Chapel Down, Austin, TX 78729
Information Systems, 1502 Norris Dr., Austin, TX 78704
Inlingua Translation Services, 9111 Jollyville Rd., Suite 102, Austin, TX 78759
Ralph McElroy Translation Company, PO Box 4828, Austin, TX 7865

Accento, PO Box 45027, Dallas, TX 75245
Accurate International Translations, Inc. 17619 Medina Dr., Dallas, TX 75287
Foreign Language Center Inc., 2909 Cole Ave., Suite 300, Dallas, TX 75204
Inlingua, 16990 Dallas Parkway, Suite 103 Dallas, TX 75248
International Translating & Typesetting Co., 2730 Stemmons Fwy., Suite 302, Dallas, TX 75207
International Translating & Typesetting Company, 2730 Stemmons Fwy, Suite 302, Dallas, TX 75207
Liaison Language Center, 3500 Oak Lawn Ave., Suite 110 LB 32, Dallas, TX 75219

Barinas Translation Consultants, PO Box 160424, San Antonio, TX 78280

Berlitz, 5815 Callaghan Rd., San Antonio, TX 78229

Summit International, 5859 Woodridge Oaks, San Antonio, TX 78249

Texas Linguistic Services, 4438 Centerview Dr., Suite 201, San Antonio, TX 78228

Trans-America, 11625 Pomeroy Circle, San Antonio, TX 78233

Translating Concepts, 2611 Country Hollow, San Antonio, TX 78209

Translation Services, 8626 Tesoro Drive, #515, San Antonio, TX 78217

Language Plus, 41 10 Rio Bravo, Suite 202, El Paso, TX 79902

Translators International, 3833 S. Staples St., #11, Corpus Christi, TX 78411

UTAH

ALPNET, Inc., 4444 S. 700 E., Suite 204, Salt Lake City, UT 84107

Foreign Translators & Interpreters, 2870 E. 3300 S., Salt Lake City, UT 84109

Multiling International, PO Box 169, Provo, UT 84603

VIRGINIA

Ampac Group, Inc., 5713 Edsall Rd., Alexandria, VA 22304

ASET International Services Corp., 2009 N. 14th St., Suite 214, Arlington, VA 22201

BBC Multilingual Translations, 1231 Somerset Dr., McLean, VA 22101

Berlitz, 2070 Chain Bridge Rd., Tysons Corner, VA 22103

CACI Language Center, 2425 Wilson Blvd., Suite 420, Arlington, VA 22201

Capcom Foreign Language Interpreter Services, 6707 Old Dominion Drive, McLean, VA 22101

CISFL, 90 Oak Forest Circle, Charlottesville, VA 22901

Diplomatic Language Services, 1117 N. 19th, Suite 800, Arlington, VA 22209

Ebon Research Systems, 45240 Business Ct., Sterling, VA 20166

Globalink, 9302 Lee Highway, Fairfax, VA 22031

Glorioso Communications, 262 Cedar Lane, Vienna, VA 22180
Inlingua, 1901 N. Moore St., Suite ML-02, Arlington, VA 22003
Languages Unlimited, 4900 Leesburg Pike, Suite 402, Alexandria, VA 22302
Languages Inc., 6201 Leesburg Pike, Suite 400, Falls Church, VA 22044
PSC, Inc., 10560 Arrowhead Dr, Fairfax, VA 22030
Statistica, Inc., 1401 Wilson Blvd, #300, Arlington, VA 22209
Word for Word Inc., 950 W. 21st St., Norfolk, VA 23517

WASHINGTON

Academy of Languages, 98 Yesler Way, Seattle, WA 98104
ACE Translation Center, 200 W. Mercer St., #504, Seattle, WA 98119
Adem's International Service, Inc. PO Box 69762, Seattle, WA 98168
Corporate Translation Services, Inc., 601 E. 22nd St., Vancouver, WA 98663
Documents International, Inc., 601 Aurora Ave. N, Suite 100, Seattle, WA 98109
Dynamic Language Center, 5200 Southcenter Blvd., Suite 5, Seattle, WA 98188
transACT, 13000 Beverly Park-Edmonds Rd., #G, Mukilteo, WA 98275

WISCONSIN

Accent Typography & Translation, 245 N. Pinecrest St., Milwaukee, WI 53208
Flagg & Associates, 759 N. Milwaukee St., Milwaukee, WI 53202
Hess-Inglin Translation Service, 4137 N. Woodburn St., Milwaukee, WI 53211
International Communication by Design, Inc. 1726 N. First St., Milwaukee, WI 53212
Iverson Language Assoc., Inc., PO Box 93306 Milwaukee, WI 53203
Jackson Graphics, Inc., lboennes W141 N9314 Fountain Blvd., Menomonee Falls, WI 53051

APPENDIX 4:

TRANSLATION COURSES AND PROGRAMS

Academic programs for those interested in translation and interpretation are in a state of flux. There is a growing recognition of the fact that the most critical need for the practicing translator is hands-on experience, albeit some of the policymakers in academia continue to cling to theory rather than practice. Programs are growing and expanding, to include many new areas. If interested in an academic program, contact one or more of the following schools and find out more about their latest offerings.

ARIZONA

University of Arizona, 1717 E. Speedway Blvd., Tucson, AZ 85719
Training for Court Interpretation.

ARKANSAS

University of Arkansas, Fayetteville, AR 72701
Literary translation program.

CALIFORNIA

Monterey Institute of International Studies, 425 Van Buren St., Monterey, CA 93940
Certificate in Translation or Interpretation.
San Diego State University, 5402 College Ave., San Diego, CA 92115
Certificate in Translation and Court interpreting.
Stanford University, Stanford, CA 94305
(415) 497-1068
Certificate Program in Translation and Interpretation.
University of California, Los Angeles, 10995 Le Conte Ave.
Los Angeles, CA 90024
Certificate in Interpretation and Translation in Spanish.
California State University, Long Beach, 1250 Bellflower Blvd, Long Beach, CA 90840
BA in Spanish translation.

California State University, Sacramento, 6000 J St., Sacramento, CA 95819
Courses in translation and interpretation.
Fuller Theological Seminary, 135 N. Oakland Ave., Pasadena, CA 91182
Translation concentration in graduate degrees.
National Hispanic University, 135 E. Gish Rd., San Jose, CA 95112
Spanish translation program.
San Jose State University, 1 Washington Sq., San Jose, CA 95192
Translation courses.

CONNECTICUT

Wesleyan University, Middleton, CT 06457
Interpreters for the Deaf Workshop

DISTRICT OF COLUMBIA

Gallaudet College, Washington, DC 20002
Only Liberal Arts college exclusively for the deaf. Offers associate degree in interpreting for the deaf.
Georgetown University, 1221 36th St. N.W., Washington, DC 20057
Certificate of Proficiency as Conference Interpreter, and Certificate in Translation in French, Spanish, German, Italian, and Portuguese.
American University, 4400 Massachusetts Ave., NW, Washington, DC 20016
Certificate in French.

FLORIDA

Florida International University, Miami, FL 33199
General translating and legal interpreting in Spanish, English, French.
Florida Atlantic University, Boca Raton, FL 33431
Course in Spanish translation.
Florida A&M University, International Translation Center, Tallahassee, FL 32307
Certificate in technical translation (literary, legal, business, medical, science and technology).

GEORGIA

Georgia State University, 1 University Plaza, Atlanta, GA 30303

Certificate in translation and interpretation.

HAWAII

University of Hawaii, Manoa, East-West Rd., Bldg 1, Rm 6, Honolulu, HI 96822
Certificate in conference interpretation.

IDAHO

College of Southern Idaho, PO Box 1238, Twin Falls, ID 83303 (208) 733-9554

IOWA

University of Iowa, Iowa City, IA 52242
Master's degree in literary translation.

ILLINOIS

University of Illinois at Urbana-Champaign, 707 S. Mathews St., Urbana, IL 61801
Courses in Russian literary translation.

INDIANA

Indiana University, Bloomington, IN 47405
Courses in Russian translation.

KANSAS

Kansas State University, Manhattan, KS 66506
Course in Spanish translation.
Johnson County Community College, College Blvd. at Quivira Rd., Overland Pass, KS 66210

MARYLAND

University of Maryland, 3106 Juan Ramon Jimenez Bldg, Colleg Park, MD 20742
Translation courses (including diplomatic translation).

MASSACHUSETTS

Brandeis University, Waltham, MA 02254
Literary translation courses.

Elms College, Chicopee, MA 01013
French and Spanish translation courses.

MICHIGAN

Madonna College, 8425 West McNichols Rd., Detroit, MI 48221
Western Michigan University, Kalamazoo, MI 49008
Technical translation courses.

MINNESOTA

St. Olaf College, Northfield, MN 55057
Courses in translation.

MISSOURI

Washington University, St. Louis, MO 63130
Courses in literary translation.

NEBRASKA

Kearney State College, 905 W. 25th St., Kearney, NE 68847
Translation and Interpretation in French, German, Spanish.

NEVADA

University of Nevada, Reno, NV 89557
Court Interpreter Seminar/Workshops

NEW JERSEY

Montclair State College, Upper Montclair, NJ 07043
Certificate/Degree program in Translating and Interpreting in Spanish
and Italian.
Rutgers, New Brunswick, NJ 08903
MA in German translation.

NEW YORK

Columbia University, Barnard College, 3009 Broadway, New York,
NY 10027
BA in literary translation.
Binghamton University SUNY), PO Box 6000, Binghamton, NY
13902
Translation research.

Brooklyn College, 2900 Bedford Ave., Brooklyn, NY 11210
Transltion courses.
City University of New York, 33 W. 42nd St., New York, NY 10036
MA in translation.
Fordham College, Fordham Rd., Bronx, NY 10458
Courses in translation.
Hofstra University, Hempstead, NY 11550
translation courses.
New York University, 48 Cooper Sq., Rm 107, New York, NY 10003
Courses in Spanish and French translation, emphasis on commercial
translation.
State University of New York at Albany, 1400 Washington Ave.,
Albany, NY 12222
Certificate in Russian translation.

NORTH CAROLINA

University of North Carolina at Charlotte, Charlotte, NC 28223
German translation program.
North Carolina State University at Raleigh, Foreign Languages, Box
8106, Raleigh, NC 27695

NORTH DAKOTA

North Dakota State University, Fargo, ND 58105
Translation courses.

OHIO

Kent State University, Kent, OH 44242
MA in French, German and Spanish translation.
Ohio State University, 1841 Millikin Rd., Columbus, OH 43210
BA in Russian translation.
Notre Dame College, 4545 College Rd., Cleveland, OH 44121
Translation program.
Antioch College, Yellow Springs, OH 45387
Workshop in poetry translation.
Baldwin-Wallace College, Befea, OH 44017
Translation courses.
Bowling Green State University, Bowling Green, OH 43403
Translation courses.

Wright State University, Colonel Glenn Hwy, Dayton, OH 45435
Translation courses.

PENNSYLVANIA

Carnegie-Mellon University, Schenley Park, Pittsburgh, PA 15213
Scientific/Technical Translation in French, German and Spanish.
Human and machine translation.
Mt. Alysius Jr. College, William Penn Hwy. Rte. 22, Cresson, PA 16630
Associate degree in interpreter training.
Pennsylvania State University, University Park, PA 16802
Graduate translation degree.
University of Pittsburgh, 1328 CL, Pittsburgh, PA 15260
Translation certificate program.
Immaculata College, Office #4, Faculty Center, Immaculata, PA 19345
Translation courses.
La Salle University, Philadelphia, PA 19141
Translation courses.

RHODE ISLAND

University of Rhode Island, Kingston, RI 02881
Translation courses.

SOUTH CAROLINA

Lander College, Greenwood, SC 29646
Translation courses.

TENNESSEE

Chattanooga State Technical Community College, 4501 Amnicola Highway, Chattanooga, TN 37406
Offers associate degree in interpreter training.
Maryville College, Maryville, TN 37801

TEXAS

Rice University, 6100 S. Main, Houston, TX 77001
Offers Certificate/Degree prograin in Translation and Interpretation in Spanish and Portuguese.

Associate degree in interpreter training.
University of Texas at El Paso, El Paso, TX 79968
Minor in translation.
University of Texas at Arlington, 7500 W. Camp Wisdom Rd.,
Dallas, TX 75236
Courses in translation.
Southern Methodist University, Dallas, TX 75275
Courses in translation.
Texas Tech University, Lubbock, TX 79409
French translation courses.
University of Texas at Austin, Austin, TX 78712
Translation courses.

UTAH

Brigham Young University, Provo, UT 84602
BA in Spanish translation.
Utah State University, Logan, UT 84322
German translation courses.

VIRGINIA

George Mason University, Fairfax, VA 22030
Graduate certificate program in translation.

WASHINGTON

University of Washington, 5001 25th Ave., NE, Seattle, WA 98195
Translation courses.

WISCONSIN

North Central Technical Institute, 1000 Schonfield Ave., Wausau,
WI 54401
Program for Interpreters.

APPENDIX 5:

TRANSLATOR ACCREDITATION

The American Translators Association (ATA) offers accreditation in 19 language pairs: from English into Dutch, French, German, Italian, Japanese, Polish, Russian, Portuguese and Spanish, and from those languages (including Arabic) into English. Once you have started to do translation in any of these languages, I strongly urge you to look into ATA accreditation. While it is not a must, it is certainly prestigious and adds professional credibility to your work.

The ATA is the main organization of translators in the United States. During my close to twenty years of association with this organization, I have seen it double and triple its membership to some 5000 translators. Its annual conference and its local chapter meetings are a wonderful opportunity for meeting colleagues and learning more about the world of translation. Its publications are very valuable tools for translators, and its monthly magazine, *The ATA Chronicle*, is a superb professional publication.

The ATA has chapters in North Carolina (Carolina Association: CATI), Missouri (Mid-America: MICATA),Washington, DC (National Capital Area: NCATA), New York (New York Circle: NYCT), Cleveland (Northern Ohio: NOTA), San Francisco (Northern California: NCTA), and Los Angeles (Southern California: SCATIA).

For more information about ATA accreditation, call or write to:

ATA Headquarters
1800 Diagonal Rd. Suite 220
Alexandria, VA 22314
tel. 703/683-6100
fax 703/683-6122

TRANSLATION GLOSSARY

Accreditation: A service provided by the ATA to confirm the competence of a translator.

Anti-Virus programs: Programs used to protect your computer and disks from destructive computer viruses.

ASCII: pronounced askey, it stands for American Standard Code for Information Interchange. It is used to save text in order to covert it from one word processing program to another.

ATA: See American Translators Association.

American Translators Association: The official organization of translators in the United States.

CD-ROM: Compact Disk-Read Only Memory - a high capacity disk for storing such information as entire dictionaries and encyclopedias.

Certification: The vouching for the completeness and accuracy of a translation by a second translator.

Conference interpretation: Interpreting with the aid of earphones at a conference at the same time the speaker of the original language speaks.

Consecutive interpretation: Interpreting each time the speaker of the source language stops speaking.

Cultural adaptation: Adapting a translation to the cultural environment of the target language.

DOS: Disk Operating System, or a program that makes a word-processor work.

Escort interpreter: An language expert who accompanies foreign visitors to the U.S. as their interpreter.

Fax: Short for facsimile. A device for transmitting printed text over the phone line from one fax machine to another.

Freelancer: Someone who works independently as a translator.

IBM PC: Or its compatible, are computers widely used by translators.

JPRS: Joint Publications Research Service, a U.S. Government agency which has historically provided a large volume of translation to freelancers.

LAN: Local Area Network, or a system of interconnected computers.

Machine translation: Or MT, refers to translation by computer.

Macintosh computers: Less used by translators than the IBM type PC.

Microsoft Word: Word processing program with good graphics capability. Not as widely used by translators as WordPerfect.

Modem: a devise for transmitting electronic text (computer files) over the phone line from one computer to another.

Mouse: a device for moving the cursor or arrow on the screen, used for operating Windows programs, as well as DOS.

MT: See Machine Translation.

Norton Utilities: A program for retrieving lost text in a computer.

Notebook: Compact portable computer.

OCR: Optical Character Reader. A card used in a scanner to transfer text from a page into word processing program.

PC: Individual computer.

Scanner: An electronic device for copying text or graphics from a page to a computer disk.

Simultaneous interpretation: Interpreting at the same time the speaker of the source language speaks.

Source language: The language one translates from.

Subcontractor: Either a translation company subcontracting with another company for translation services, or a freelancer subcontracting with a translation company or any other entity.

Target language: The language one translates into.

Translation Bureau: Same as translation company.

Translation Agency: Same as translation company.

Translation company: A company which provides translation services, and subcontracts with freelancers.

Verbatim translation: Complete translation of every word of the original text.

Voice-over: Taping a translated text for audio or video media.

Windows: An operating system for PCs that is more versatile than DOS, especially with graphics.

Word count: The method of arriving at a total words in a given text for the purpose of determining the cost of the translation.

WordPerfect: The prevalent word-processing program among translators in the U.S.

WordPerfect Foreign Language Module: WordPerfect-based software for different languages and alphabets.

INDEX

American Translators
Association (ATA) 32,36,39,
40,82,117,118
Arabic 5,12,14,15,25,41,56
CD-ROM 25,28
Chinese 5,12,25,41,58
Commerce Business Daily 89
Computers 2,7,13,19,22-26,28
30,47
Dictation 11,12,23
Dictionaries:
  Arabic 56
  Chinese 58
  English 52
  French 62
  German 65
  Hebrew 69
  Italian 71
  Japanese 73
  Portuguese 75
  Russian 77
  Spanish 81
DOS 24
Embassies 34,38
Exceller 25
Fax 2,7,12,19,24,25,30
French 5-7,12,21,25,27,41,47
German 5,6,12,25,27,34,35,
41,65
Hebrew 5,25,28,69
IBM 24
International
corporations 37,40,41
Interpretation:
 Conference 45
 Consecutive 45
 Escort 46
 Simultaneous 45

Italian 5,12,25,29,41,71
Japanese 12,25,28,34,
35,41,73
JPRS 38
Laser printer 26,42,49
Law firms 31,33,34,37,40,41
Macintosh 24
Microsoft Word 25
Modem 2,7,12,19,24,25,30
National Geographic Society 40
NATO 47
Networking 39
Norton Utilities 119
OCR 26
Optical Character Reader 26
PC 23-24
Portuguese 25,41,75
Printers 26,49
Resume writing 42
Publishers 34,35,39
Purchase order 33
Russian 12,21,25,26,34,41,
48,77
Scanner 26
Scientific American 17
Source language
9,10,15,16,20,45
Spanish 5-8,12,18,25,27,28,
34,35,38,41,81
Target language 9,10,14,16,
27,40,45
Translation:
 accreditation 117
 Bible 6
 companies (bureaus, agencies)
  35,36,38
 freelance 22,25,28,30,31,33-
 39,42

getting paid for 12,31,33,40
legal 11,20,37
literary 1,14,47
machine 47-48
misconceptions about 13
rates 31-32
speed 11,19,23
study programs 43
technical 1,11,13,14,21,
    22,23.27,28,30,
    34,43,45,48
Wall Street Journal 17
War and Peace 21
Windows 24-25
Word count 12
WordPerfect 22,25-26
Xialibaren (XLBR) 25
Yellow Pages 36